Sea Captains of Cape Cod

Each Town's Contribution to Maritime History

Michael V. Pregot

LOCAL HISTORY PRESS

an imprint of Sunbury Press, Inc.
Mechanicsburg, PA USA

LOCAL HISTORY
PRESS
an imprint of Sunbury Press, Inc.
Mechanicsburg, PA USA

For information about special discounts for bulk purchases, please contact Sunbury Press Orders Dept. at (855) 338-8359 or orders@sunburypress.com.

To request one of our authors for speaking engagements or book signings, please contact Sunbury Press Publicity Dept. at publicity@sunburypress.com.

FIRST LOCAL HISTORY PRESS EDITION: March 2022

Set in Adobe Garamond Pro | Interior design by Crystal Devine | Cover by Lawrence Knorr | Edited by Lawrence Knorr.

Publisher's Cataloging-in-Publication Data
Names: Pregot, Michael V., author.
Title: Sea captains of Cape Cod : each town's contribution to maritime history / Michael V. Pregot.
Description: First trade paperback edition. | Mechanicsburg, PA : Local History Press, 2022.
Summary: From its earliest roots of indigenous fishing, to the puritans landing at Provincetown, through the American Revolution, during the glory days of the "Great Age of Sail" and eventually to worldwide shipping and passenger travel, Cape Cod can claim a major role in each aspect of American maritime history. The personal stories of the courageous men and women who made it happen deserves a chance to be heard. Every Cape Cod community can boast of famous and some lesser-known seafaring figures who made the ocean world their personal home.
Identifiers: ISBN : 978-1-62006-877-9 (softcover).
Subjects: HISTORY / United States / 19th Century | HISTORY / State & Local / New England (VT, CT, MA, ME, RI and NH) | BIOGRAPHY & AUTOBIOGRAPHY / Historical.

Product of the United States of America
0 1 1 2 3 5 8 13 21 34 55

Continue the Enlightenment!

Contents

Foreword

Whether you are a long-time resident of Cape Cod, an official "washashore" living on the Cape for decades, a frequent tourist, or merely someone with a lively curiosity about this unusual stretch of beachfront property, you will find information to spark your imagination. Enjoy this compilation of intriguing biographies of famous and lesser-known Cape Cod captains and naval figures.

Along the way, sidebars will cover many points of appeal that may spark your interest. On the following pages, you will find:

- Cape natural history and geography.
- A town-by-town description of its history and development.
- Important maritime connections for each town.
- The origins of significant geographic names.
- Historic visits made by American presidents.
- Naval engagements in several wars.
- Maritime history.
- Early American history.
- A history of the indigenous people.
- Female perspectives on life at sea.
- The uncovering of some lesser-known yet significant maritime figures.
- A resource guide for further maritime research.
- Entrepreneurial endeavors that were popular in the early nineteenth century.

This book is designed for both leisure reading and the formal student of maritime research. A thematic foundation is established for each town to trace its general history and rapport with the ocean and a tribute to the people who made their living connected to the sea.

Introduction to Cape Cod's Maritime History

People, particularly along the Eastern seaboard, simply call this region of Massachusetts "the Cape." Of course, there are several other famous capes as we make our way down from Maine to Florida. Speculatively, an earlier name for Cape Cod can be traced back to a Viking voyage. A Great Northeaster storm accidentally blew Bjarni Herjulfsson off course on his way to Greenland. In 986, he was bound for the Viking colony founded by Eric the Red. When he reached land, he was told of the land to the south. He referred to this place as Keel Cape due to the similarities of his Viking boat to the physical shape of the shore.

Six centuries later, in 1602, Bartholomew Gosnold, an early Cape explorer, had an inkling to name the region Shoal Hope (Shallow Harbor). However, his crew saw the ocean teeming with "fresh Cod." This abundance of cod was so plentiful that they could almost be scooped by hand on the side of the boat. His crew convinced him to change his mind. Hence, this stretch of land, jutting prominently out into the Atlantic Ocean, acquired the name of Cape Cod.

The area known as today's Cape Cod is a product of centuries of natural evolution. It exists as the result of the advance and retreat of the Laurentian Continental Ice Sheet. This gradual rise and fall of an ice sheet saw a rise in sea level followed by a constant retreat. This reconfiguration of land mass occurred over twenty-five thousand years, verified by radiocarbon techniques. It explains how kettle ponds were created and how ocean beach contours expand and recede. It even provides a valuable hint as to the future extinction of Cape Cod.

Approximately twenty-three thousand years ago, the massive glacier had reached its furthest advance, including the islands of Nantucket and Martha's Vineyard. The ice sheet itself is comprised of various lobes that created large basins within the bedrock surface of the earth. The western side of Cape Cod was formed by the Buzzards Bay lobe, while the middle portion came to be called the Cape Cod lobe. The lower or outer cape became known as the South Channel lobe, which occupies a large basin on the east side of the cape. During its initial point of creation, the entire landmass was comprised of glacial ice.

The ice remained a prevalent fixture until the last fifteen thousand years, when partial incremental melting resulted in land shaping. Geologists note this land transformation process as a recent evolutionary footnote within the grand scheme of multiple millenniums of geologic development.

Today, the two existing Cape Cod bridges are the exclusive means for any vehicle to seek entrance and egress to this site. The current peninsula shape of Cape Cod only became a fully developed manmade island once the Cape Cod Canal was finally constructed. The canal itself came as a passageway for faster and safer transfer of goods over maritime waters. Concurrent to the canal emergence, a need for an overarching bridge to span traffic over the canal became necessary. So, both the Bourne and Sagamore Bridges were erected between 1935 and 1940 as a WPA (Works Progress Administration) project. An original pre-existing bridge with a 100-foot width was further expanded to a length of 480 feet was eliminated. There is currently a discussion of two new bridges to replace the two structures that have significantly aged.

In geographic terms, Cape Cod Bay is a barrier island, one of the largest in the world, shielding Boston and the rest of Massachusetts from the strong North Atlantic storm waves. On the grand scale of overall physical land growth, Cape Cod is assuredly losing gradual land mass each year. The shorelines change dramatically every year, with nuanced growth in the summer followed by greater erosion in the winter. The cape typically loses a minimum average of 4,400 acres of land mass annually.

The degree of absolute land erosion depends upon in which community you live. On the Atlantic side, towns such as Eastham and Orleans lose about two and a half feet of the seashore, while on the bayside, loss of land in towns such as Dennis at Chapin Beach and Yarmouth is up to ten feet each year. Sandwich's Town Neck Beach is now seen as an erosion hotspot with many storm surges, ocean flooding and high waves noted within the past five years. Over the centuries, this man-made land mass has achieved a special status. It is revered for its natural beauty, beloved for its active range of geologic activities, yet always appreciated for its ability to blend natural land mass within a historic setting.

Before we embark on our maritime voyage, we should reflect on our first round of Cape Cod residents. The first stage of history would be the displacement of the indigenous people who lived on the Cape shores for centuries. In subsequent chapters, we will briefly discuss where and how early European settlers established their local land claims.

Our Earliest Residents—The Indigenous People

The most prevalent indigenous group of people was the Wampanoags. This group of people is a loose confederation of several tribes, speaking a variance of the Algonquin language. Two of these tribes have been federally recognized, the Mashpee Wampanoags and the Wampanoags of Gay Head. In addition, Massachusetts has recognized the tribes of Herring Pond and the Assawompsett-Nemasket band living near the Mattapoisett and Rhode Island region.

For the most part, the Wampanoag people were stationary in their settlements with only occasional seasonal movements between summer and winter housing. The men often traveled far from home, searching for seasonal fishing and larger mammal hunting. They frequently stayed away for weeks or months at a time. The women cultivated three major varieties of vegetables, namely maize, climbing beans, and squash (called the three sisters) as the staple foods for their diet, supplemented by any fish or game contributed by the men. Each local indigenous community had authority over a well-defined land territory assigned to them from which the people sustained life. The land was apportioned in terms of a per family "wetu" (hut) as a plot of land and separate tribes residing in different geographic locations.

The indigenous people were living here for centuries before the Europeans arrived. Some of the sister tribes, all affiliated with the Wampanoag, living here had names such as the Nausets, Namasket, Pocassets, Manamoynicks. Shawme or the Pamet people. Tribal authority existed primarily along matrilineal lines. The men engaged in building relationships with other tribes and defending their families in times of war while the women ran the local community.

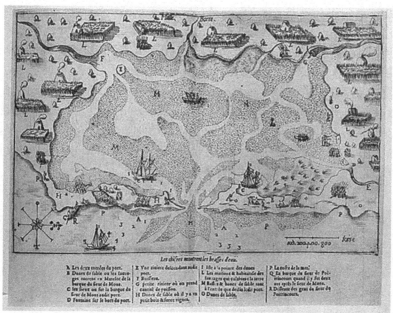

Champlain's drawing of Plymouth Harbor, 1605. (Courtesy of National Park Service.)

The Wampanoag people were, at heart, a matrilineal system in which women-controlled property. Any hereditary status was passed through a maternal line to either a male or female. The marriage agreements were also matrifocal. When a young couple married, they lived with the woman's family. Women elders were the decision-makers who approved the selection of the chiefs or sachems. Men acted mostly in political roles to build relationships with neighboring tribes and served as defenders in times of war.

Food production among the Wampanoag was similar to many Native American societies, with food habits divided along gender lines. Men and women had specific tasks. Women played an active role in many of the stages of food production and processing, so they had important sociopolitical, economic, and spiritual roles in their communities. Wampanoag women took care of farming and gathering wild fruits, nuts, berries, and shellfish. They were responsible for up to seventy-five percent of all food production in Wampanoag societies.

The Wampanoag were loosely organized into one confederation in which one head sachem held sway. The colonists considered the head sachem as a king, but the position of a sachem differed from kingship in many ways. First, they were selected by women elders and were obliged to consult with their councilors within each tribe. A petty sachem may exist in a specific region, while the head sachem was the generic accepted leader. Head sachems were also responsible for arranging trading rights and protecting their allies in exchange for some form of material tribute. Both women and men could hold the position of sachem, and women were frequently chosen over their closer male relatives.

On rare occasions, elite men were permitted to take several wives for political or social reasons because multiple wives symbolized great wealth. Women were the producers and distributors of corn and other food products. In their culture, marriage and conjugal unions were of lesser importance than were the ties existing between clan and kin.

Much of the local geography still maintains the original Wampanoag names on street signs and maps like "Potenumacut" (round rock) or "Hokum Rock" (bending back) or Saquatucket Harbor (tidal river). Some of our current vocabularies can be traced back to the local Algonquin-speaking people. Examples of English word adoptions include opossum, squash, skunk, and toboggan. The term "Massachusetts" itself (large hill place) is derived from a Wampanoag tribe residing near the Blue Hills Reservation in Milton.

Eventually, there would be a blending of European and indigenous people. Five years before the arrival of the *Mayflower*, starting in 1615, English sailors conducted raids along the present-day New England coast, grabbing mostly young men for slavery bringing them to European investors. One such captured native, Tisquantum (commonly called Squanto), was captured and brought to Europe but returned to his homeland by sympathetic Spanish religious figures. An amazing turn of events marked his return to the Cape. European sailors unwittingly spurred an unfortunate viral infection spreading among the natives taking the lives of the vast majority of the local Wampanoags from 1616 to 1660.

Realizing Squanto wished to be reconnected with his native roots, his compassionate host of Spanish monks agreed to release him to go home. Upon arrival, Squanto learned that his entire local tribe never survived their smallpox-like viral epidemic. All had perished. He eventually found a new tribe willing to adopt him. By the time. the *Mayflower* landed, there was an utter surprise for the Pilgrims coming across an English-speaking local native who could serve as translator for them and provide the newcomers with information on basic survival skills. He so enjoyed working with pilgrims that he requested an English-style burial upon his own death. It is believed that his remains are now buried directly on the Eastward Ho Golf Course in Chatham.

The extremely high mortality rate of more than half of the indigenous villages coincided with the Pilgrim's arrival. These two connecting events became a major factor to simplify the process of acquiring Cape Cod land. Since the head sachem ceded negotiation rights to their local sachems, dealing with a smaller local leader facilitated many territorial acquisitions. These land deals also needed to be officially filed within the newly emerging colonial courts and, in some cases, with the Court of Saint James in England.

There is a traceable record of land receded to the local tribes, by the Europeans, mostly in today's Mashpee. Richard Bourne succeeded in securing 10,500 acres reserved for Native American use. In 1762, Reuben Gogenehew traveled to London to convince the court of Saint James to affirm the territory for recording the land for the local indigenous people.

During the American Revolution, the Native people needed to pick sides. Many sided with the British, hoping more land could be reclaimed. Other indigenous people became so bonded with their newly arrived immigrants that they volunteered for the Colonial Army. By the time of the War of 1812, most natives fought with the British. We know that over seventy Native Americans from Cape Cod alone lost their lives while fighting bravely in the cause of the American Revolution. No matter which side was selected, the native people recognized their own culture would be lost.

Despite previous written and oral agreements to the contrary, American courts often rescinded indigenous rights. By the year 1788, most lands were lost. In 1834, Mashpee itself became a free-standing district. Thirty-six years later, it was incorporated as a town. In the 1970s, the Wampanoag tribe attempted to sue the federal government to recognize land rights within the town. The struggle to fully recognize the Wampanoag tribe as a legal entity with lawful rights remains a contentious unresolved battle.

Our second installment of the history of Cape Cod is the European advent. Their story is discernable in the chronology of each town becoming officially incorporated. Our second historic saga reflects how the territory was officially re-apportioned within the colonial culture. By establishing the authority of the state and local courts to handle land disputes, an official legal process emerged. Complicating matters in Colonial America was an obligation to file all land decrees with the Royal Court of Saint James in London.

Three points should be highlighted as far as maritime history goes concerning the Wampanoag. The women were responsible for the coast harvest. They would gather in the mussels, quahogs, and oysters, and any beached fish specimens that might come their way. There is evidence that a larger dugout constructed by men on occasion would go out in search of larger fish. Also, the Wampanoag family tribe in Aquinnah acquired skills in whale hunting. Their chief would lead a religion-inspired ceremony known as the "Powdawe," pursuing the large mammal in the open ocean, chanting as their capture was brought to shore.

Drawing of Indigenous tribes by Deyo, 1898. Simeon Deyo, History of Barnstable County 1620–1637.

TABLE 1. The Chronology of Cape Cod Towns

Ranked by Date of Town, Incorporation	Town Name	Year of First European Settlement	Name Before Incorporation	Official Year of Incorporation
First settlers from Saugus relocated	Sandwich	1637	The Indigenous name was Shawme	1639
Tied for 2nd Oldest	Barnstable	1639	Indigenous name was Mattacheese	1639
Tied for 2nd Oldest	Yarmouth	1639	Yarmouth Included Dennis	1639
Fourth	Eastham	1644	Eastham included Orleans and Wellfleet	1646
Fifth	Falmouth	1661	Saconesset Part of Barnstable	1686
Sixth	Harwich	1688	Included Brewster	1694
Seventh	Truro	1670	Truro Locals called it Pamet	1709
Eight	Chatham	1656	Monomoit	1712
Ninth	Provincetown	1714	Meeshawn called Hell Town in the early 1800s	1727
Tenth	Wellfleet	1694	Eastham	1763
Eleventh	Orleans	1644	South Parish of Eastham	1797
Twelfth	Dennis	1639	East Precinct of Yarmouth	1793
Thirteenth	Brewster	1653	North Parish of Harwich	1803
Fourteenth	Mashpee	1639	Oldest spelling was Marshpee, In 1763, Mashpee Plantation	1870
Fifteenth	Bourne	1637	Sandwich	1884

Which Cape Cod Community Holds Title to Being "The Official Sea Captains'" Town"?

A major purpose of this book is to examine the degree of each Cape Cod town's contribution to seafaring life. Many towns from different eras have claimed that their specific town has a unique edge to the title, "The Home of the Sea Captains." Should only one specific town assert unique mastery of the sea, or might several communities commonly share in this contentious heritage? In truth, it was discovered that each town indeed has a unique connection to the sea, and perhaps each town should be given some recognition for its efforts.

Maritime historian Henry Kittredge referenced this very debate eighty-seven years ago:

> For rivalry pure and simple, nothing in the history of sail was ever keener than the feelings between captains who came from neighboring towns on the Cape. To the citizens of 'High Barnstable' the rest of the cape was unworthy of serious consideration. Brewster, even today, takes backwash from no one on earth; Provincetown from the days before the Mayflower always has been a law—and sometimes no law at all-unto itself: Dennis realizing complacently that her list of deep-water captains was a proud one, looked upon other Cape shipmasters as little more than fishermen: Yarmouth defied any town in the county to show finer captains than the Eldridges, while Eastham and Orleans, secured by Hatch and Linnell, were content to let Sandwich boast its Ezra Nye , and Truro point proudly to the Collins boys. (*Shipmasters of Cape Cod*, 1935, p. 179–180)

To continue with the evidence of the extensive maritime connections from each Cape Cod town, we will cite a specific Barnstable County court case in 1825. Daniel Webster once wrote to a friend living in Dennis about a compelling trial held in Barnstable Court. Since geographic familiarity was a critical concern to the legal issue at hand, he described in detail the Sandwich Islands going into minute depth about the harbor of Owyhyhee in the Pacific. He noticed a broad smile beaming across the faces of several jury members. He asked the question, how many of you men have seen this harbor? To his amazement, seven of the twelve jury members present responded affirmatively and, in fact, have seen it several times during their ocean travels.

Relative Physical Size of the Cape Cod Communities

Cape Cod towns come in all sizes and shapes. Being a string of coastal towns, a great deal of our local history is directly formed in relationship to its degree of shoreline shapes and beach access.

TABLE 2. Cape Cod Towns Ranked in Terms of Their Geographic Size

Name of Town	Square Miles – Land/Water	Ranked Size Order
Barnstable	62.74	First
Falmouth	45.72	Second
Sandwich	43.62	Third
Bourne	41.54	Fourth
Mashpee	25.96	Fifth
Yarmouth	25.53	Sixth
Brewster	25.16	Seventh
Harwich	22.41	Eight
Dennis	21.90	Ninth
Truro	20.82	Tenth
Wellfleet	20.82	Eleventh
Chatham	16.33	Twelfth
Eastham	14.60	Thirteenth
Orleans	14.19	Fourteenth
Provincetown	8.75	Fifteenth

When you start to examine the relative size of the various Cape communities, you gain a deeper appreciation for its history, industrial growth patterns, and appreciation for what small towns can do.

Henry David Thoreau described the physical contour of Cape Cod as a human arm flexing it into a muscle. "Cape Cod is the bared and bended arm of Massachusetts. The shoulder is at Buzzard's Bay; the elbow at Cape Mallebarre (Chatham) the wrist at Truro; and the sandy fist at Provincetown."

Selective Review of Maritime Figures

Selecting the precise number and name of maritime figures to represent each community was a most arduous task. Even though hundreds of potential mariners were worthy of consideration, only five representatives per town were chosen as a reasonable limit for an informed yet brief overview. Admittedly, the selection was extremely subjective in scale and substance. This collective description of the chosen mariners provides a representative sample of Cape Cod life through several centuries, all related to the sea. Direct communication with the towns' historical societies and a study of literary works suggested by local public librarians were of immense assistance to the author to create the list. The spirit of shipmasters, shipbuilders, sea captains, sailors, and commercial traders come alive with every story told.

Barnstable County Court House built in 1832. (Courtesy of Wikipedia, by Zirkel.)

Barnstable

Origin of the Town's Name

Barnstable takes its name from "Barnstaple" (an older spelling) in Devonshire, England. In terms of its natural contour, its harbor appears similar aesthetically to its European namesake. There is a large ocean flat area amid its harbor generated by the ebbing and flow of the receding ocean. Hyannis, one of the Town of Barnstable's seven villages, takes its name from a corrupted version of the name Iyanough, a friendly sachem of the Cummaquid tribe of Wampanoag Indians.

The French name given to Barnstable Harbor confirms the presence of abundant shellfish, as witnessed by Samuel de Champlain. He initially named it "Le Port aux Huistres," or Oyster Harbor. It is theorized that many of the early residents came either directly came from Barnstable, England, or could trace their familial lineage back to that same European site.

A Brief History

Barnstable is one of the first three Cape Cod towns, officially incorporated in 1639. Initially, this region was divided into two basic divisions. One area served as a military demarcation for militia training, while another served as the religious parish. It grew slowly but steadily into various clusters of homes. Eventually, villages were formed. Near Cape Cod Bay, Barnstable and West Barnstable villages bordered the ocean. Moving into Nantucket Sound, Cotuit, Osterville, Centerville, and Hyannis were established along the Long Island Sound. Finally, nearer to Mashpee, the village of Marston Mills was established.

In 1637, Parson Joseph Hull and a small group of his parishioners, apparently unhappy with their Weymouth setting, resettled just east of the boundary of Sandwich. In October of that same year, Reverend John Lothrop arrived with a large membership of Congregationalists. The Lothrop settlement grew in prominence and incorporated itself as the Town of Barnstable. The original configuration of Barnstable included land called Saconesset, which, in 1686, became incorporated and later in 1693 changed its name to Falmouth.

At first, the young town of Barnstable was most prominent for its agriculture and animal breeding. Later, residents branched out to include fishing and melded other trades into their economy. Shore whaling thrived with a try-works built to process blubber in several locations. Barnstable was nearly devoid of any hardwood trees in the early 1800s as all of its local wood was needed to construct tryworks (blubber furnaces). In the early 19th century, there were no less than 804 different ships harbored within the town.

Notable Connection to the Sea

Evidence of a strong maritime history exists in Barnstable in several forms even today. Three of the largest sea-faring harbors on Cape Cod are located here. Barnstable Harbor on the northside is a natural open sea harbor used for centuries for commercial shipping and private boating. Today whale watching trips and multiple boat launches are seen. Hyannis Harbor is also a natural setting on the southside for sunset cruises, Hy-Line Tour boats, and the Steamship Authority take cars and passengers to Nantucket and Martha's Vineyard. While Lewis Bay, smaller in scale, is a dredged harbor. It can be thought of as the center of the triceps when visualizing the "arm" of the Cape. Counting the sheer number of ships harbored here between 1820 and 1840 would seem to require significant effort and diligence as hundreds of ships could be documented.

Henry Kitteridge (1935) revealed the challenge of the scope of maritime research on Cape Cod, "A glance at the various villages in the town of Barnstable will convince anyone of the hopelessness of doing justice to so large a subject as maritime searches. More than eight hundred names appear in the list of Deep-Water shipmasters, even this catalogue is by no means complete (Shipmasters, 1935)."

CAPTAIN WILLIAM STURGIS (1782–1863)
A Fortune Seeker Extraordinaire

Born in Barnstable to William E. Sturgis and Hannah Mills, Sturgis had an illustrious maritime career. William was a ship master and a lineal descendant of Edward Sturgis of Yarmouth. Edward was the first member of the Sturgis family to arrive in America in 1630. He holds a distinction among Cape Cod sailors as he can claim participation in three of the most lucrative trading ventures, the Northwest Fur Trade, the California Hyde Trade, and The Chinese Merchant Trade.

In 1796, William joined the counting-house (financial record-keeping office) of his uncle Russel Sturgis. He entered the family business through marriage as an in-law. His sister, Elizabeth Perkins, was the wife of Russell Sturgis. Upon his father's death in 1797, he went to sea to support the family as an assistant trader on the *Eliza*. He served as the first mate of the *Ulysses,* serving under Captain Charles Derby on the *Caroline* until the very day that Derby died at sea.

In the summer of 1798, he was provided mate training aboard the *Eliza*, a smaller vessel of 136 tons. His wages were a comfortable seven dollars per month to serve as a "green hand before the mast." As the title implies, a novice mate would be given basic first mate chores and assigned other duties such as cleaning, scrubbing, organizing, cooking, or other manual labor required on a long ocean voyage.

In 1804, his experience led to commanding the *Caroline,* sailing from the Columbia River to Kaigahnee, south of Prince of Wales Island, Alaska. On this one trip, he acquired no less than twenty-five hundred sea otter skins netting a profit of $73,034. His logbook indicates that the value of sea-otter pelts in the China Trade increased steadily almost every year during the early 1800s. Originally, each pelt sold for thirty to forty dollars in Canton. Later in that same century, pelts could be sold for over one thousand dollars due to their diminishing availability and demand. It is estimated that in 1804 alone, more than fourteen thousand pelts were traded by American ships.

Sturgis knew that gaining the trust of the indigenous tribes was an initial key to building a strong personal bond and gaining confidence with the indigenous natives. He accomplished this goal through a study of their dialect. Indeed, he took this task most seriously. He analyzed several local indigenous dialects, becoming fluent enough to communicate with ease with various tribes. His local notebook often recorded local words written in phonetic scribble. He also demonstrated a moral tone by venturing into deeper discussions on local customs while offering his viewpoint to the natives on appropriate religious studies.

His linguistic research was directly documented in a historic "first edition" type of indigenous dictionary in his ship log. At the end of each journey, he added a glossary of native words taken from the local tribes of Caigenee or Kigarnee. He referred to these two distinct languages as Sheeta or Sitka. Although fairly rough, he formed words using a basic phoneme creation. He was able to preserve a language that up to that point was only known as an oral dialect, previously never formally recorded.

He was, by all standards, a modest youth. In his log, he once mentions an elderly native woman he referred to as Madame Connecor. He stated that he had absolutely no possible escape but was forced to submit to being kissed and hugged by her in public. This overt activity seemed untoward to his sensibilities, yet he endured it. Since the woman was an influential member of a local tribe with many connections, he agreed to her touch to promote future trading ventures.

As a sea captain in his twenties, his moral reputation was evidenced by being asked to serve as a judge. While on the Northwest coast, he once approached the ship *Ulysses* anchored nearby. The ship had recently undergone a mutiny. With the assistance of Captains Rowan and Breck, two other nearby captains, a decision was made to board the mutinied ship to determine if justice could be meted out. The three captains agreed that the original captain was unduly harsh to his crew yet could remain as the leader if he swore to refrain from cruel, unreasonable ways. Most of the crew voluntarily agreed to stay aboard, but the current ship's mates immediately removed themselves from the brutish captain and abandoned the ship.

By June 1806, Captain Sturgis was twenty-four and was now able to become one of the premier sea traders in the Northwest and China sea trade based on his acquired maritime skills combined with his skill in native languages and his ability to arrange amicable agreements.

In 1809, his ship, the *Atahualpa*, was attacked by Chinese pirates while moored at Macau Roads. Sturgis managed to get the ship underway and fought off the pirates using four small cannons he had brought on board, directly against the expressed wishes of the ship's owner. Sturgis had been prepared to blow up the ship if the pirates caught them to save the crew and passengers from being tortured. The ship's owner, Theodore Lyman, first reportedly chastised Sturgis for violating his direct order to bring cannons on board, then realized their very presence saved the day. He was extremely pleased. All seemed well that ended well.

The Atahualpa, *ship of William Sturgis. (Courtesy of Barnstable County Records.)*

Under the protection of the canons, he managed to fight just long enough to sail within the range of friendly support guns aimed from the harbor. The pirates were eventually captured. Their commander, Appotesi, was later tortured to death by the Mandarin authorities. He was executed through a painful process known as "*the thousand cuts*," a tortuous and languishing manner of death.

After his maritime days ended, his wealth and prominence brought him to a new career. He served as a Massachusetts congressman, both in the house of representatives and the senate. He was consistently known to have voted for what he believed to be the "correct, moral, and right" thing to do compared to obeying any single party-led conviction.

JOSIAH RICHARDSON OF CENTERVILLE (1808–1853)
A Most Moral Sea Captain

At the tender age of twenty-one, Josiah Richardson became master of the schooner *Hetty Thon*. He made his first deep-sea voyage in the following year, sailing from Boston to Cronstadt near St. Petersburg, a major trading center, commanding the brig *Orbit*. He roamed the oceans with his cousin George Richardson of Boston for the next nine years, primarily aboard the brig *Owyhee*. On some trips, he would bring lumber from Cuba to Russia and then return with Russian fir used to construct elegant American homes.

His first assignment of ships was of a relatively smaller dimension than his competitors. In 1839, he took command of the *Chatham*. This ship was a particular favorite of his as it carried almost double the weight of his previous vessels. He frequently brought cotton from the Southern United States ports and delivered it to Liverpool or Le Havre, often stopping at Cuba to secure rum. Speaking of rum, in one specific instance when the remains of a deceased passenger started to decompose without alcohol aboard, he was said to have hailed a passing British vessel to purchase a keg of rum for its use, keeping the decaying body intact for the remainder of the trip.

While in command of the *Walpole*, he took copious notes on various dangers that lurked in front of the sea captains during that era. In 1847, his log recorded: "Heavy gales from N. W. and rough seas. Squalls, snow, and hail. Tried using the pumps without success, the ship laying down so much upon her board side the water would not come to them at all."

Despite all the meteorological challenges facing him, he sailed the *Walpole* across the Atlantic in twenty-eight days. Even with an inventory of mostly broken and inoperable nautical instruments at his disposal, he brought the *Walpole* back to Boston safe and sound. His maritime skills were deemed legendary. When he learned that his next assignment was to go to Manilla, he was delighted. Wishing warmer climates, he looked forward to seeing new tropical ports.

His logbooks reported with great pride that "The *Walpole* arrived at its destination to the straights of Sundra which separates Java from Sumatra in record time. Our passage has been ninety-five days, rather short, as the vessels that sailed before us have never noted such a wonderful time."

While in Manilla, it took four months to secure all his desired cargo, loading sappan wood, hemp, manila, rope sugar, buffalo hides, and sugar. Securing those items which would return a reasonable profit. It was always a carefully considered risky enterprise to buy items on impulse compared to purchasing only a set menu of heavily demanded items. Sea captains needed to become shrewd entrepreneurs developing a keen sense of which exotic items would best appeal to the public.

Between 1812 and 1850, there were four major recognized types of deep-sea captain operations: (1) general trade with Europe, (2) transatlantic passenger travel from Boston or New York to Liverpool, (3) long sea voyages to China and the East Indies and (4) finally the advent of the clipper trade from local ports from Cape Cod to Boston and beyond. Captain Richardson was one of the few shipmasters who participated in all four types of these maritime excursions.

Since his ships would most often carry both cargo and passengers, additional challenges were inherent in that duality. On one occasion, the voyage between Boston and Liverpool was filled with a crew of "Liverpool Irishmen" notorious for their devil rum drinking and expert skills with a knife. Deep knowledge of human nature was the handiest trait to possess. Keeping the crew in full control and on their best behavior while still making the trip enjoyable for travelers required a delicate reflective balancing act.

The captain needed to be firm with sailors without seeming overbearing. He allowed consumption of rum only up to a fixed limit, even enjoying a small libation himself with the crew. He always served as an example of proper behavior. His demonstration showed how rum could be enjoyed and consumed within moderation. He exemplified cordiality to both crew and passengers throughout the voyage.

In 1849, many medium-sized clippers traveled the ports around Cape Cod. Master shipbuilder Donald McKay designed a ship recognized as a nautical design wonder, the class of the fleet. Her name was the *Staghound*. She possessed lines that had the maritime world abuzz with envy. She was the largest and most revered ship of that century. With the appointment of Richardson as its captain, he immediately became the hero of the shipping world.

Before taking command, a celebrated underwriter Walter Jones questioned his wisdom. "With such a ship of great weight, so heavily sparred and for so long at sea, are you not nervous?" His response was: "I would never go on any ship at all if I ever for a minute I suspected that it would be my coffin."

While on its inaugural launching, the main mast of the *Staghound* broke in mid-voyage. He composed a note to his owners, "The ship is yet to be built that would beat the *Staghound*. I am perfectly in love with her. You have reason to be proud of her. I shall get a new main-topmast, take in in my water and leave here for San Francisco." True to his word, a record travel time was recorded even with the time wasted for an emergency repair.

A letter written by the American Ambassador to Russia is proof of the integrity and international respect that people held for Captain Richardson. The letter was a congratulatory note memorializing heroic efforts by Richardson traveling out of his way to save a Russian captain. In all, there was a crew of eleven sailors stranded upon a stranded boat during the ocean. Not knowing exactly where to send the letter, the ambassador first sent the note directly to Daniel Webster, the Secretary of State. Webster then brought the note to the Customs Office at Boston, which forwarded the laudatory message to the captain.

To further cite the humility of the respected captain, his log for the precise day of the rescue was composed without fanfare at all, "Came across a small ship of nine Russian men. Took them on board lamenting that one of their men, the ship's carpenter, was lost at sea." In short, the local mariners of his era frequently referred to Richardson as the maritime model, par excellence, suitable to guide the proper behavior for all future sea masters.

DANIEL C. BACON (1788–1856)
An Intrepid Barnstable Sea Captain

Bacon was the first mate of Sturgis when the *Atahualpa* was attacked in Macao. He would become the next great Barnstable sea captain to distinguish himself in the Northwest and China Trade. He earned a reputation as a fighter at an early age. A group of young men once accused him of being a "bushwhacker," which at that time was a term used to denigrate a poor person coming from a rural area possessing a strident attitude. He was verbally assailed by a group of drunken sailors impugning his integrity. Rather than just accept their taunt, he plotted a way to use his horse in retaliation. He returned within an hour on horseback, galloping through their midst, causing them to fall into the mud. His feisty reputation added a new measure of respect for a captain who would not be criticized.

A letter from his father, written to him in 1810, shows the rather vast connection that Barnstable sea captains enjoyed with the China trade. While in command of the *Atahualpa* preparing to return home, his father wondered: "How many other Barnstable boys shall you carry after taking Asa Jenkens and Joseph Crocker's sons?" He replied: "There is half of the boys in this town that mean to go on my next voyage."

While on Canton during the war of 1812, his ship was frozen in the harbor as an embargo was pronounced on American ships. One night, with a fresh breeze behind him, he slipped into the darkness. His pilot, a local Chinese citizen, begged to set him ashore. To safely gain release from the harbor, he kept the pilot on board until all was safe, dropping the citizen into a smaller boat to return when all was calm.

His China trade route earned him great profits establishing an excellent business reputation. In 1818, he took a year off to regain his health. He temporarily retired, lost some weight, and filled a sorely missing empty part of his life. He embraced a new wife.

Theodore Lyman, a wealthy shipping merchant, commissioned him once again to sail the ship *Alert*. This jaunt would be his final voyage. He was hampered in his pursuit by his strict business orders. Lyman insisted that he only purchase silk at a certain price. Due to the extreme competition, the asking price exceeded his order. Nonetheless, he loaded his ship with tea and local silk products rushing home before his competitors could follow. Despite his original orders, his intuitive spirit and sharp business sense were rewarded with a healthy profit.

As president of the American Navigation Club, he challenged British maritime officials. He offered a prize of $50,000 to the first ship that could leave Boston to arrive in China and then return. There were no restrictions on the weight or the type of ship used. Unfortunately, this race never occurred as many suspected that American shipbuilding was far superior to any other country in the 1820s.

He retired from the sea, moved to Boston with his family, and became a prosperous merchant and owner of thirty ships. He built Bacon Farm on Main St. in Barnstable as a summer residence. He died in 1856.

CAPTAIN JAMES BACON CROCKER (1804–1883)
Mandated Sunday School at Sea

Born in West Barnstable in 1804, he was thirty-three years of age when he took command of the *Eben Preble,* one of the finest East Indiamen sailing out of Boston with a half dozen Cape Cod men by his side. Being quite pious, he insisted his crew participate in a regimented Sunday service. He wanted both their minds and souls to be nourished as they sailed the globe.

A full range of religious instructions and skill-based activities were scheduled for the holy Sabbath. At first, a full chapter was read from the New Testament. It would then be interpreted and discussed based on the crew's interpretations. Next, the religious aspect of the service would conclude with prayers led by the seaman's devotional assistant. Temporal skill-based activities would then follow. There would be courses in knot-tying, sail-making, preparing "sennit" (braided cordage in flat, round, or square shapes used for making lashings), or in the carpentry needed for nautical blocks).

For further safety from looming pirates in the Sundar (Indonesia) region and other unsavory areas, the crew would prepare loaded cartridges, taking turns practicing musket marksmanship. He was consistently known for exercising extreme caution. When half of the crew would go inland to seek new provisions, a partial crew was left armed on the ship, ready for any invasion. His firm belief was the speed of the voyage was never the most critical factor but rather that the mission progressed as planned.

On one trip, he dropped anchor heading for a site located 156 days outside of Boston Harbor. He took a full week to load cotton and other merchandise, packing the vessel to its fullest. His trademark utilized a series of smaller cargo runs with immeasurable attention to cargo quality. This five-month trip to complete was quite profitable, making the owners proud of the authoritative flexibility given to the captain.

Nineteen days after this voyage, he set sail for the other side of the world, heading for Calcutta. On this trip, rats infested his ship. There were thousands of them teeming on the deck, finding their way into the many cargo holds. He led a "Pied Piper" drill in which all rodents were driven off the ship lead by tempting them with morsels of food, avoiding costly and bloody extermination.

He was a competent shipmaster, not a mere brutal driver, concerned only with wild haste, nor was he an idle master. You were well-educated and protected from harm's way when you were aboard his ship. With his next assignment, he assumed command of the ship *Oxnard* in 1840. He would travel to China and the East Indies for the next twenty years.

By 1860, he moved from his birthplace to the neighboring town of Yarmouth, where he retired to a distinguished career of public service for his new community. He opened a large store at the corner of 6A and Willow Street, which unfortunately was consumed by fire a few years into its operation. A Bed and Breakfast Inn now stands today where his family once resided.

JOHN PERCIVAL (1779–1862)
Mad Jack Percival, the Savior of *Old Ironsides*

He earned the title of "Mad Jack Percival" during the War of 1812. While in command of the *Peacock*, he set out on three military excursions in

1814. He captured nineteen merchant vessels and two British Warships on those three trips. Congress rewarded his efforts by raising his rank to Lieutenant and presented him with a sword of valor. He was a celebrated officer in the United States Navy in one war and five different naval excursions, including a small skirmish with France, the War of 1812, the campaign against West Indies Pirates, and the Mexican-American War.

Born in Barnstable, Percival left his Cape Cod home at thirteen to work as a cabin boy on a trading vessel traveling along the East Coast. He transferred his lessons learned from merchant sea service to the military. As a youth, he was impressed by the British Royal Navy while his ship was moored in Lisbon. First, he was sent to the HMS *Victory*, serving under Lord Jervis. He next received an assignment to a captured Spanish merchantman vessel. Predicting a severe lack of discipline among his crew, Percival survived a mutiny, escaping to the American merchant ship *Washington*.

Once again, impressment would change his life. This time, his new captives would become part of the Dutch Navy. Managing to escape a second time, he decided in 1799 to put his naval knowledge to use by enlisting in the United States Navy. Subsequently, he served in a smaller obscure war with France as a master's mate. There he rose to the rank of midshipman. Finally, he was discharged in the demobilization of 1801, returning to merchant service.

In 1838, once again, he was asked to serve the needs of his country. He took command of the second-class ship sloop the USS *Cyane*, headed towards the Mediterranean, partnering with Commodore Isaac Hull. His duty involved educating and training a new generation of young midshipmen. Percival took to this task with eager passion.

Many prominent men with midshipmen sons commonly asked for their youngsters to be trained by Mad Jack. Many of his students went on to distinguished naval careers. Citing one example, Gustavus V. Fox continued to become Lincoln's assistant secretary of the navy. John L. Worden, a *Cyane* midshipman, became an admiral and is remembered as the hero of Hampton Roads.

Another trainee Captain Henry Wise once noted: "There is not a better sailor in the world than Captain Percival or a man of better judgment in the qualities requisite for a seaman. I would rather trust my life to his charge in case of emergency at sea than any other man in the United States Navy." Percival eventually retired from the *Cyane* late in 1839 due to poor health. He received a promotion to captain in September 1841, the highest U.S. Navy rank.

He started an even more memorable chapter of his life in November 1843. The venerable frigate, the USS *Constitution*, was a major question mark for the United States Navy. The older ship served as a barracks for Navy staff. Constructors estimated that it would cost $70,000 to refit her for sea when funds were sparse. Acting Secretary David Henshaw, from Massachusetts, knew about Mad Jack's reputation for frugality.

USS Constitution, *also known as* Old Ironsides. *(Courtesy of US Naval Archives.)*

Percival reported he could complete the work for $10,000. Despite serious doubts about Percival's promise, Henshaw awarded him the task. This renovation project worked, keeping an American treasure, *Old Ironsides*, sea-worthy for future generations.

Upon completion of his restoration project, Percival was then directed to carry the first U.S. ambassador to Brazil on the USS *Constitution*, proceeding to the east coast of Africa and then moving on to the China seas, making a return to the United States. He left New York at the end of May 1844. Before the voyage ended in Boston 495 days later, his renovated ship sailed 52,370.5 miles, a distance equal to circumnavigating the globe two times as a notable and proud chapter in her long and illustrious career.

Bourne

Origin of the Town's Name

Some people might incorrectly think its name "Bourne" flows from one of the very first settlers in that area, Richard Bourne. Richard was an original pioneer, a popular and well-known farmer, and a minister and advocate for the indigenous people.

A second more authentic origin of the town's name stems from a businessman, Jonathan Bourne. He was an affluent whaling merchant in the 1800s and a civic philanthropist. Through his business acumen of sponsorship of whaling expeditions, he acquired enormous wealth. His daughter demonstrated her generosity by donating land, and financial endowment to civic causes led to the construction of several town structures such as the First Memorial Library.

A Brief History

The first European presence arrived shortly after the Pilgrims established Plymouth Colony. Within a few years, the Colony was trading goods with the Dutch settlers of New Amsterdam, meeting near Bourne Village. In 1627 they built a trading post at Aptucxet, a replica of which sits today on its original foundation. In 1640, the first recorded settler from Plymouth Colony was Ezra Perry, who obtained land officially noted as Sandwich during that era.

Two men from Sandwich were the originally assigned missionaries for the indigenous people in this region, Richard Bourne and William Leveridge. Richard Bourne was born in 1610 in Devonshire, England. He was only twenty-four when he settled in Saugus, later named Lynn. Being a close friend of Pastor William Leveridge, he was among fifty families choosing to settle in Sandwich in 1637. Pastor Leveridge was a lover of Jesus and a lover of people. He was a student of the indigenous languages, soon mastering several dialects to spread the good news of the gospel. He also could solve disputes. Both traits were passed on to his disciple, Richard Bourne, his next-door neighbor. When Leveridge left Sandwich for Long Island in 1654, Richard Bourne continued preaching for decades to convert indigenous people.

Before the pilgrims arrived, this area was referred to by the local people as "Manomet." This term can be translated as "a gathering" of the native people." When an issue of appropriate unfair taxation arose in the early 1880s, residents from the villages of Bourne, Bournedale, Buzzards Bay, Sagamore, Monument Beach, and Pocasset separated from Sandwich to appoint their selectmen, seeking an independent voice. It was the final town in Cape Cod to be officially incorporated.

Notable Connection to the Sea

In 1627, English colonists from Plymouth Colony established a trading post twenty miles south of Plymouth at Aptucxet on the Manamet River (also known as the Manomet). The post would become the colonists' first permanent settlement on Cape Cod. This trading post on the Manamet River area would trade pilgrim provisions for corn and beans, supplying food to the newcomers to the land. The name Aptucxet is of Wampanoag derivation, meaning "little trap in the river," referring to a fishing trap located in the river.

The post was established primarily to trade with the Wampanoags. The colony relied on their local harvest while still desiring a fur trade to repay local debts owed to England. The trading post also increased trade between the English colonists and the Dutch colonists of New Amsterdam to the south, today's New York City.

Aptucxet was the original trading post established by the Plymouth colonists. It was followed in 1633 by the Metteneque Trading Post in Windsor Locks, Connecticut, and the Cushnoc Trading Post in Augusta, Maine. Aptucxet was located a considerable distance from the main colony. It was staffed year-round by colonials. A horrific hurricane, passing through in 1635, damaged the main building. The post was ultimately abandoned by the 1650s. The land later became part of a large farm. The current replica building on the site today was constructed with the assistance of archeologists using federal funds in 1935.

Later, the Manamet and Scusset Rivers were widened early in the 20th century, leading to the formation of the Cape Cod Canal. This new route closely followed a similar route to the one used by Plymouth colonists traveling to the post. Consequently, the Aptucxet Trading Post Museum is now located on the banks of the Cape Cod Canal rather than on the Manamet River.

It is noteworthy to mention that the Massachusetts Maritime Academy, originally founded by an act of the Massachusetts Legislature on June 11, 1891, as the Massachusetts Nautical Training School, is also located in Bourne. The name was later changed in 1913 to the Massachusetts Nautical School, and it took its present name in 1942.

JONATHAN BOURNE (1811–1888)
Instrumental for the Presidency of Abraham Lincoln

His family instilled honesty, integrity, bluntness, and a strong sense of generosity into the young man as a youth. In this section of Sandwich (called Bourne today), the length of time a teacher shared with his students was a direct corollary to the family's contribution of wealth to the community. In Jonathan's situation, his part of town had the services of an instructor for 113 days in a year.

At the age of seventeen, Jonathon shared time between his studies and serving as a grocery clerk in the largest store of its day. His first-year store duties consisted of basic menial tasks such as sweeping, waiting on customers, replenishing stock, completing inventory checks, and maintaining the books for his employer, Mr. Webster.

He managed to save just about every penny he ever earned and quickly saw that greater wealth could be acquired in ways other than being a local farmer or even working as a grocery clerk. Analyzing the potentially profitable enterprises of the day, he correctly predicted that whaling soon would become a booming industry. His first investment resulted in purchasing a 1/16 share of a whaling ship, the *General Pike*. His return on investment was more than favorable. He realized the immediate growth

Jonathan Bourne

factor. So, the subsequent year, he acquired a one-fourth share of the ship, *Roscoe*, for $1,925.

By 1836, he dismissed all aspects of the grocery business and ventured full-time into the whaling investment profession. He acquired a full interest in ten more ships within three more years. Initially, he saw that for an original investment of $180,450, he could turn a profit of $73,013 annually, which equated to a 41% rate of return. By 1839, he was well on his way to seeing a profit of over one million dollars per year. He could approach an earning rate of over two million dollars in a good year. He expanded his empire to include a Fire Protection Services division for a short time. Feeling a civic duty, he used his wealth and influence to enter politics as an alderman in New Bedford.

In a well-known family feud with his brother, he struggled in civil court to challenge the distribution of his father's will. Rather than merely squandering funds to a brother who he believed was indolent, he had the courts agree to reduce the annual claims of his brother. He then applied these same funds towards other civic projects. The local people admired his inherent instinct for shrewdness and blunt confrontation of facts. His business empire continued to expand. By 1876, he ascended to President of Merchant's Bank, which became the primary lending institution of its day.

After his wealth was well established, he became a prominent political figure in local and even national affairs. Originally named the Whigs, his party affiliation would later change to the National Republican Party. He was welcomed with open arms. In 1860, he was elected as a Massachusetts delegate to the Presidential Primary Convention. When a close electoral contest unfolded between Seward and Lincoln, his influence, personal persuasiveness, and promise of wealthy support carried significant weight into the contest. Today, many pundits agree that his support was perhaps the prime motivational factor carrying Abraham Lincoln to the presidential nomination.

He later became a central figure in the Western Railroad Movement. His reputation now extended well beyond the Bay State. He was seen as a forceful national figure. He ran for a congressional seat, being elected to the first district congressional district formed in Southern Massachusetts. He would eventually retire to the Bourne area of today and was instrumental in establishing parks, libraries, and schools in Bourne. His wealth, compassion, business skills, and complete dedication to community needs were principal reasons that his name arose when this section of Cape Cod pulled away from Sandwich.

GEORGE BAULDRY (1824–1889)
The Stowaway Who Became Captain

Captain George F. Bauldry, son of Samuel Bauldry, was born in England in 1824. Striking out on his own to seek a new and adventurous life, he risked both life and limb by settling in as a stowaway on a ship captained by Nathaniel Burgess. Captain Burgess discovered the youth hiding in blankets and took compassion on him. With his wife, Anna, he took pity on the youth, formally adopting him. He was raised in the Burgess family home. As a youth, he quickly acquired maritime skills, working as a cabin boy in his preteen years. He accompanied Captain Burgess on several whaling trips along the Eastern shores.

Records indicate that he was mostly at sea during a half-century between the years 1836 and 1888. Nonetheless, he did find time to marry Nancy Berry in 1853. He had three children: George, Ella, and Lyman. Although primarily a whaling captain, there is evidence that he helped the American cause in the civil war by creating the Stone Fleet.

The Stone Fleet consisted of a group of aging ships, mostly whalers purchased in New Bedford, that were physically loaded with stones. These ships then sailed south during the Civil War by the Union Navy to be used as a naval blockade. They were deliberately loaded with hefty weights and then sunk at the harbor entrance of Charleston, South Carolina.

This blockade intended to obstruct various naval runners, supplying Southern interests with needed cargo during the Civil War. Some of these stone ships accidentally sank along their route, while others were sunk near Tybee Island, Georgia, serving as breakwaters. Wharves were then built upon them for the landing of the Union military.

This flotilla of ships was divided into two lesser fleets. One fleet was sunk to block the south channel off Morris Island, and the other blocked the north channel near Rattlesnake Shoals off the present-day Isle of Palms. All this work proved to be a dismal failure as blockade runners could navigate around them into the main shipping channels of Charleston Harbor. George Bauldry eventually retired to his home

Union naval blockade during the Civil War. The Stone Fleet, a failed experiment. (Courtesy of US Navy Archives.)

in present-day Bourne in 1888 but unfortunately died a year later. He earned a solid reputation as a patriotic hero and a superior mariner.

WILLIAM (1819–1855) AND HANNAH REBECCA BURGESS
A "Self-Proclaimed" Sea Captain

One might wonder how a female might take command of a merchant ship in the mid-nineteenth century. One possible way of doing so is first to marry a sea captain, display a keen interest in how sailing ships operate and then accompany your spouse on several year-long journeys. In 1852, Hannah Rebecca married William Burgess. She would cross the equator eleven times while serving as a willing apprentice for the next three years.

She claimed to have sailed as the master of the *Challenger* from the Pacific to Boston at the age of twenty-two as her husband took fatally ill, finally dying of dysentery. Although, there is now specific documentable evidence within her journal that refutes the accomplishment. She describes her facts in such vivid detail in her memoir that they seem believable. Unfortunately, a subsequent critical review of her notes contradicts her story as the primary navigator.

Our maritime story is also intimately aligned to the life of William Burgess. As a competent first mate, it is no surprise that he was commissioned command of his first ship, the *Herbert,* at the age of twenty-two. The ship was slow but steady and most certainly was rigged to handle a voyage to Asia and any other port in the world. Captain J. Henry Sears, his employer, recognized his talent, confidently concluding he would thrive as a captain.

In his maiden voyage of the *Herbert,* there were technical difficulties with the compasses, all facing diverse directions. Using the binnacle compass as a baseline, he determined the correct direction to head. He made the journey from Boston to Calcutta in one hundred and fourteen days, considered an exceptional time. With a strong will and solid resolve, he made the return trip in only one hundred and eleven days compelling his company to be quite pleased with his achievement. He boasted in his ship's log, "So ends the voyage of the *Hebert* in record time for the day."

In 1855, he acquired command of the clipper *Challenger*. By 1856, the ship arrived in California. Burgess was commissioned to visit the

Chincha Islands off Peru to pick up guano (bat dung), highly prized by farmers for its rich nitrogen base used in various parts of the world.

The problem with this cargo was two-fold. It was a highly flammable substance when placed into a confined location, and two, it was deemed extremely hazardous to breathe. Unfortunately, this trip proved overwhelming, with the captain falling extremely ill. Since the nearest medical expert was a twenty-two-day sail away and the captain could not function, time was against them. The captain finally succumbed within two sailing days before reaching a doctor.

Hannah Rebecca wrote about taking command of the ship in the voyage's final leg, taking her husband's body back for burial at the Sagamore Cemetery. She returned to the family home in Bourne where she lived, refusing several marriage proposals later in life. Her fiercely independent spirit contrasted sharply with the accepted norms of the Victorian women living in this era. Whether or not she uniquely mastered the ship halfway around the globe, it is certain that she stuck to her claim for decades and equally certain that the local people within her community greatly respected her as a heroine.

Image of the Cincha Islands, London Times, *1863.*

PETER STORMS (1769–1837)
The Blockade Runner in South America

In 1802, Napoleon Bonaparte attempted to recruit as many young men as possible to fight in his army. Peter's mother negotiated a fee for his passage to take her young son to the United States to escape this fate. So, Peter was abruptly swept up to New Bedford when this site was bustling with commercial and whaling fishing ventures. He quickly became enamored with a life at sea.

Peter was given command at a very young age of a ship trading in South American-made products. This period represents the same era that most Central and South American countries sought independence from Spain. His normal trading pattern included frequent trips where his ship, traveling from Boston to Maracaibo, needed to avoid Spanish-controlled blockades to deliver and transfer their wares.

His skill as a blockade runner came to the attention of General Simon Bolivar. Storms was commissioned to bring supplies and military arms to support Bolivar's fight for South American independence. Even though Bolivar's army had won the internal land battles in several countries, Spain still had a firm hand in dominating the seas.

To bolster his help with naval intervention, Storms received financing to build a speedy schooner in Connecticut provisioned with cannons. The *Peacock* joined the rebel fleet and served its purpose by delivering needed supplies into the hands of the revolutionaries. This risky, dangerous venture came with many rewards. His earnings associated with Bolivar were such that he could purchase over three hundred acres of land that included Rocky Point and the Grey Gables area of Bourne.

On July 24, 1823, thanks to his maritime skills and daring, he once again broke a blockade. The Battle of Maracaibo forced Spain to surrender, ending Spanish domination. He captured a Spanish warship, the *Liberal,* when his crew boarded waving machetes, forcing sailors to flee for their lives. Total control of the seas was now in Bolivar's favor.

His recompense was enormous. Indeed, upon one visit to a New Bedford bank, there were so many golden Spanish coins deposited that bank officials insisted that legitimate evidence be required to authenticate the deposit. This proof was obtainable with the funds deposited.

Captain Storms continued his trading adventures beyond this period with the partnership of another local seaman, Ebenezer Nye. As an expert in South American business and with important political connections, his value as a maritime blockade consultant for both the Venezuelan and American trade placed him in great demand.

GEORGE BRIGGS (1843–1909)
Civil War Hero and Fishing Guide for Grover Cleveland

George was remembered as one of the town incorporators of Bourne. As the Barnstable County Commissioner, a fishing partner of President Grover Cleveland, a library trustee, and the first school committee chairman, he carried significant local influence. George I. Briggs was instrumental in incorporating Bourne as a town in the Massachusetts courts. His revered naval career during the Civil War propelled him to prominence and public recognition.

In 1861, at the age of eighteen, citing his occupation as a fisherman, George enlisted as an ordinary seaman into the United States Navy. Records indicate that he served his country on several vessels. The *Ohio* set sail from the Charlestown Navy Yard. Then, the *North Carolina* sailed to the port of New York. Next, the USS *Sumpter* consumed his ocean and fighting skills through most of 1862. The *Fernandina* would become the ship that employed his longest assigned time.

He wrote several times in his journal of his love of the *Fernandina*. The vessel was informally named *Florida*. In one journal excerpt, he has just paid a visit to another ship, saying: "Comparing these two ships, this one is nothing to the Fernandina." In another passage, he writes: "The Fernandina looks as neat as a pin since she has a new coat of lead paint, looking like a new craft."

In his logbook aboard the *Fernandina*, he describes his "picket duty," which consisted of staying on deck during the dark hours of the night to spot "greyhounds," which was the local euphemism for blockade runners seeking entry through the restricted area. He eventually would rise to the rank of quartermaster. The quartermaster is the enlisted member in charge of the watch-to-watch navigation and the maintenance, correction, and preparation of nautical charts and navigation publications. They are also responsible for navigational instruments and clocks and training ship's lookouts and helmsmen.

On January 16, 1864, George proved his valor. A confederate sloop was spotted in an inland creek. When the ship ran the boat ashore, the crewmen from the *Fernandina* took possession and proudly hoisted the

Stars and Stripes up the mast. After the war, he returned to his hometown community, where he prospered in business and fishing ventures. His devotion to civic duty, his work ethic, and his general knowledge of Cape Cod fishing endeared him to President Grover Cleveland, serving on board as his fishing ship guide and friend. He was seen fishing regularly at the summer White House with the president.

Grey Gables, summer White House of Grover Cleveland.

Brewster

Origin of the Town's Name

Brewster was named in honor of Elder William Brewster, the first religious leader of the Puritans at Plymouth Colony. He was a distinguished writer and orator and a leading proponent of the Puritan movement. One of the main goals of Puritanism was to clean away the Roman Catholic practices from the Church of England. When the passengers of the *Mayflower* landed at Cape Cod, Brewster became the senior elder, serving as the religious leader for the colony. He served as an adviser to Governor William Bradford. Brewster's son Jonathan joined the family in November 1621, arriving at Plymouth on the ship *Fortune*, and daughters Patience and Fear joined him in July 1623.

As the only university-educated member of the colony, Brewster assumed the unofficial post of the colony's moral and spiritual leader. Thereafter, he continued to preach until his death in April 1644. "He was tenderhearted and compassionate for those in misery," Bradford wrote, "but especially of such as had been of good estate and rank and fallen unto want and poverty."

A Brief History

The town separated from Harwich in 1802 for two principal reasons. First, the local First Parish (Puritan) Church on the bayside of the Cape believed that their share of maintenance for total church affairs was excessive. Secondly, there was also a strong political belief in this area. Many affluent shipmasters held an anti-federalist view, demonstrating their feelings of independence. Federalists favored an overall national approach, while anti-federalists opposed any heavy national intrusion.

The northeastern section of Brewster was called Setauket, and the south-eastern region was known as Namskaket.

When originally settled, the town's history developed around the Stony Brook region, called Factory Village. Here, the first water-powered grist and woolen mill in the country were founded in the late seventeenth century. The grist mill area was natural for several local shops, such as farm produce and a tannery.

Notable Contribution to the Sea

In his 1920 book, *Cape Cod Stories*, Joseph Lincoln wrote nostalgically about the prominence of the town of Brewster in maritime lore. repeating the words of Thoreau wrote in the mid-1850s, "there are more masters and mates of vessels from Brewster than from any other city of the world." We certainly can observe from its early origin of the town that captains of great note such as Cobb, Freeman, and Clark all felt the town should separate from the First Parish Church in Harwich to claim its independence.

Today, former sea captain homes adorn Route 6A and Lower Road, offering a small vestige of a most romantic era. Many of these residences have been converted to Bed and Breakfasts. The town's maritime heritage is also kept alive with various sea captains assigned to each of the 36 holes at the two town's public golf courses, Port (left side) and Starboard (right side), with the entire complex called *The Captains*.

In his book, *Cape Cod*, Henry David Thoreau offers the following entry:

> Late in the afternoon, we rode through Brewster, so named after Elder Brewster. Who has not heard of Elder Brewster? Who knows not who he was? This appeared to be the modern-built town of the Cape, the favorite residence of retired sea-captains. It is said that "there are more masters and mates of vessels which sail on foreign voyages belonging to this place than to any other town in the country."

It is unclear if Thoreau is directly quoting from an exact historic reference or merely emphasizing a generally accepted fact accepted at that time.

Packet boat travel was a very popular form of travel in the first half of the nineteenth century. Passengers looked forward to a sea voyage to Boston. Most towns on the Cape Cod Bay side had several options. There were other physical concerns in Brewster, a town without a harbor. Ocean travel along the north shore section depends strongly on tidal influences. The beaches look like any other at full tide, but the water flows back and forth at ebbtide until it leaves two miles of clean white sand, interspersed by weed-boarded channels called the flats. The packet boat could only leave at the highest tide or on a rising tide. At anchor, all boats must be in water sufficient to keep them afloat. For this reason, about a hundred yards from the high-tide mark, a breakwater was built made from natural stones abounding in the area.

Excavators had to dig a hole adjacent to the length of the breakwater itself. The incoming tide would fill the hole, leaving a space for a ship to enter on the lee side of the breakwater, the side nearest the shore. The breakwater was a mile from the beach at Cannon Hill. On that hill was a tall pole attached with a beacon. When the packets came to town, the beacon was hoisted, alerting residents to board quickly.

ISAAC CLARK (1761–1819)
Opened Up Travel to the White Sea

Being a thrill-seeker and always searching for new adventures, Captain Clark disregarded the more traditional and established ports of Europe to see what the extreme northern seas might have to offer. In 1800, he ventured up the Baltic Sea through the Gulf of Finland, facing extreme cold and more artic conditions into the Russian port of Kronstadt. This was quite a daring and bold move as he had yet received official permission from any government official to even be in that region.

He was the very first American sea captain to enter the White Sea. Once there, he needed governmental clearance to discharge and take cargo aboard his vessel in that region. Since he needed authorization from the American Ambassador, a long trek was in order. He needed to traverse through frigid Archangelsk for the more culturally rich metropolis of Saint Petersburg.

Being impetuous and daring, he feared that too long a wait might freeze his ship, the *California,* in place. He secured a local heavy-duty sleigh and whisked to the ambassador's residence at Saint Petersburg as quickly as he was able to do so. He must have indeed been a persuasive and charming spokesperson as he did indeed convince officials to grant navigational rights to a completely unknown upstart sea captain after the trip was already made.

His successful meeting and convincing personality opened a new pathway for maritime travel in the northern region. He returned to his ship and loaded it with valuable Russian fir timber. This wood was in high demand in North America due to its unusual color, flexibility, shape, and adaptability for home construction. If you decide one day to pass the captain's home on Stony Brook Road, you can still admire this stately Georgian-style mansion, with the fine Russian fir trim distinctly displayed.

Later in his life, the call to the sea, combined with the urging of his life-long friend, Captain Cobb, beckoned him out to the deep sea once again. This time, he paid dearly as it claimed his life. He was asked to head along the African Coast to trade in the highly popular and seductive commodities of oils, palm trees, gold dust, and ivory tusks. Although vehemently denied by Cobb, his sponsor, and other sea captains as the motive. It was known that slave traders would frequent this specific region of Africa.

His final inglorious fling was ill-fated as the sickness of Africa's Black Water Fever was forever present. Like many other Brewster captains before and after him, he never returned. His body was eventually buried on Africa's Prince Island, so far from the Cape Cod town that he represented for many years. It was said that Captain Cobb, for many years thereafter, felt a deep regret at coaxing this most honorable fellow captain to a location that he at first did not want to go with the earnest premonition that so much potential danger existed.

ELIJAH COBB (1768–1848)
Witnessed the French Reign of Terror

Without a doubt, one of the most noted and colorful of the Brewster Sea Captains was Elijah Cobb. He engaged with Barbary pirates, witnessed the guillotine of a legendary revolutionary figure, charmed foreign governmental officials into the payment of retribution, chaired the town's negotiation of paying the British ransom to save Brewster's saltworks, and became a preeminent negotiator for trade with Europe. After these exploits, he served his local town as their state senator and even spent time as Brewster's town clerk.

Born on a small Brewster farm, he was forced to leave home at the age of six due to the death of his father, who perished at sea. Being adopted by another maritime family, his life at sea commenced as a cook and cabin boy. As a very responsible and grateful youth, he frequently sent funds back to his mother to provide her with daily sustenance.

As a crew member of early cargo runs to Europe, he understood the Dey of Algeria was sponsoring pirate attacks on American vessels. The First Parish Church often held special collections to fund the ransom of local sailors." To the shores of Tripoli" was an early battle cry for the marines. To avoid the spot of frequent pirate incursions, he once took his ship via the north of Spain route leading him to another adventure. His was one of a hundred ships gathered by French forces while they quarreled with British forces.

On one trip, he saw his full cargo being scuttled from his ship, the *Jane,* by the French to feed their army. Being a businessman with panache and extraordinary courage, he took the bold stance of ordering his ship to return to homeport with the first mate in command. Meanwhile, he ventured to the interior of Paris to secure payment. Armed with pistols, he carefully scampered through the French countryside to reach a high-ranking Parisian official. He wrote a note to no one less than Robespierre requesting an official audience. His wish was granted.

The revolutionary leader was himself in deep turmoil at the time and reluctantly agreed to pay. Cobb witnessed the very heart of the French Revolution. Finally, he was able to obtain and then take the "paper" commitment for funds to another set of French officials who compensated him for his entire bill of lading which included a hefty profit.

For several subsequent days after this agreement, the Reign of Terror continued throughout France as the stark steel blade of the guillotine sliced through many an unprotected neck. Within a few more days, Robespierre, who ordered the deaths of so many, was guillotined himself. Cobb's eventual return to his homeport was equal to the welcome of a naval and business hero.

His skill as a navigator through the war-torn space of Europe made him much in demand as a negotiator with foreign nations. Upon taking command of the ship, *The Monsoon*, he realized that his precious cargo included a large shipment of New England rum. His trading acumen told him that Ireland might be the perfect country to pay top dollar for his cargo. This was the riskiest proposition at that time. Britain declared that all alcoholic spirits sent to any part of the British Kingdom must come from an approved English plantation.

As the ship landed near Cork, he appeared "aghast" to learn that the locals attached the King's Seal to the whole of the spirit consignment. The Irish contingent carried the prized merchandise to shore with a wink and a nod. Captain Cobb acquired a small fortune both through his ingenuity and outright bribery.

His ship, *William Tell*, was seized by the British during the War of 1812, and he would be briefly imprisoned. During the war, he stayed at home bound by great anger and angst that a British navy could threaten his country's local sovereignty. In fact, as a town representative, the British demanded a "tribute "of $4,000, or they threatened that the sound and fury of cannons would ensue upon the town's salt works. Since the local citizenry did not have access to accessible funds, the burden of payment fell upon three local merchants who eventually agreed to assist.

After this war, he resumed his maritime adventures along the African coast. His fortune grew because of these trips to the Dark Continent. However, his good luck expired when he commissioned Captains Clark, Nickerson, and Mayo to partake in this expedition. The ship, *Ten Brothers*, was consumed by African fever leaving seven men and an eleven-year-old cabin boy dead. The entire ship was eventually fumigated, filled with disease, and burnt.

He stayed in Brewster and eventually committed to a more genteel life. He established a small farm and concurrently served as an elected official serving in many capacities, such as a senate representative for two years, a state representative for eight years, a selectman for two years, and the town treasurer for ten years. It seems most appropriate that in 2017, his stately residence on Lower Road has become the home of the Brewster Historical Society containing many valuable artifacts of the Brewster Sea Captains.

La Guillotine, 1793. Engraving of nine executions, artist unknown.

TULLY CROSBY (1809–1891)
A Significant Family Lineage of Maritime Captains

Many sea captains sprang from the lineage of the Brewster Crosby clan. To cite a few whose last name was Crosby, we can mention Benjamin, Charles, Clanrick, Edmund, Elisha, Freeman Senior and Junior, Joshua, James, James E., Joshua, Nathaniel, Tully Senior and Junior, and William and Zenas. There were seventeen registered Crosby shipmasters, with eleven dying within forty-nine years of each other. These brave and adventuresome seafarers crossed the far corners of the oceans and the countries of the world, but they all hailed from their hometown of Brewster.

Just like most of the maritime families before him, Tully signed up as a thirteen-year-old cabin boy to learn the ropes from his sea captain father and then worked with his half-brother, Joshua, for the next ten years in his destined career. Beyond these first travels, he became well known for his exploits with the Chinese trade. The acquisition of various teas from China was most desirable by British importers. In 1850, he took cargo to Canton and Macao, bringing aboard spices, teas, and delicate chinaware.

Then in 1851, he became master of a brand-new ship, the *Antelope*, taking her halfway around the earth. His intended stops included Boston,

San Francisco, Shanghai, back across the Pacific, around Cape Horn, and finally, New York harbor.

His success at taking out a ship on her maiden voyage with untested navigational equipment displayed confidence and skill, which established his sailing fame. The smoothness of the trip, the length of time per voyage, and the financial gains realized made him a highly sought-after captain. He was given a second ship, the *Kingfisher*, for its initial ocean spin two years later.

This time, the inaugural voyage came with a severe challenge. Captain Donald McKay, the designer of the fine clipper ship *Bald Eagle*, wagered that he would arrive at San Francisco before his new ship. As the *Bald Eagle* left port, the *Kingfisher* was delayed for almost two full days due to technical reasons. Never having a predisposition towards failure or gloom, he took to the race with great gusto. He then made an incredible time to the California shore.

The one thing that all sailors accept as being out of their control is the capricious nature of the wind. As he was practically in sight of the San Francisco Harbor, he felt powerless as his ship was unmoved for five full days due to the caprices of nature. Nonetheless, once the winds picked up, he darted to the harbor to see his rival being in proximity.

The two tall ships entered the port within an extremely short distance of each other with the *Bald Eagle* at the rear. The able captain then brought his boat back to New York City to a hero's welcome with marine merchant experts impressed with his fine showing. Reaching this high note, the captain decided to sail no more.

Not tempting fate any longer, He returned to Brewster for a long and prosperous retirement at the age of forty-five. He was elected to local town, county, and state offices. His persuasive oral powers were strong as he convinced several seafaring peers to serve in local government. He was elected twice to the town's selectman office in 1856 and 1865.

Many other former sea captains served Brewster well. In the 1870s, Captain Snow kept the Brewster village grocery. Captain Cobb served as the town clerk. Captain Nickerson repaired the meetinghouse. Captain Baker endowed the library, and Captain Foster was the chairman of the town selectmen.

Artist rendition of the Antelope, *captained by Tully Crosby, artist unkown.*

WILLIAM FREEMAN (1820–1911)
The Captain with Many Lives

In terms of longevity both as an active and retired sea captain, it would be difficult to match the exploits of William Freeman. His earlier ships would include the *Maria, Maine, Undaunted*, and *Kingfisher.* He worked with brigs, ships, and clippers. He always knew that Brewster would be his final port-of-call in life.

To this end, in 1842, he acquired dense hardwood lumber from Alaska and intricate oriental-style rugs from France to grace his soon-to-be constructed home on Lower Road. Although it seems ludicrous to bring timber from such a distant foreign port, the availability of suitable lumber was severely limited. His home still stands today as one of the finest examples of Beds and Breakfasts in the local area. Rather than retiring at an age that many sailors thought prudent, his career would span several more decades.

He, too, became victim to the dangers of transporting coal across the ocean. While on the ship the *Mogul*, in 1874, his cargo spontaneously combusted. For many days, the entire crew faced the flames with courage and dire concern for their very lives. He was desperately hoping to reach the shores of Hawaii intact. The fires raged for over two weeks

They eventually had no option but to abandon ship and flee to their lifeboats. The ominous prospect loomed that the nearest port was still over one thousand miles ahead of them. Divine providence heard their plea as a trading schooner headed for San Francisco rescued them in the open sea. They eventually reached American shores safe and sound.

In 1859, he engaged in another immense struggle. The crew of the *Undaunted* mutinied. He was deeply wounded in a clash with his hostile sailors. He feigned death, laying in a side boat to keep himself alive. Once again, an act of divine intervention interceded. As his mutinied ship docked at St. John, New Brunswick, his crew was captured and turned over to the U.S Consul. Canadian officials saved him.

His voyages continued with trips aboard the *Monsoon, Ocean King, Jabez Howes, Zenobia, Palmyra*, and *Edward Everett*. One reason why the names of these ships so often overlapped with diverse captains at the helm was that Captain J. Henry Sears was the principal proprietor of the shipping line. He would often assign vessels to a range of captains as he saw fit to do based on availability and the individual captain's skills

J. HENRY SEARS (1829–1912)
Captain Responsible for the Provincetown Monument

In a sense, any aggregate group of sea captains can only have one true master. J. Henry Sears was perhaps a captain above his peers. He was a maritime student, a successful shipping line magnet, a recorder of history, a distinguished author, and a true philanthropist leading community action to get things done.

It does seem ironic to associate a nineteenth-century sea village with the sport of golf, but J. Henry was not only proficient in that sport, but he could also lay claim as architect and contractor to the town's earliest golf course situated on thirty-two acres of land on Lower Road with a fine clubhouse and separate bowling alley. Given his connection with the shipping giants of the day, it is most likely that the course was mostly frequented by many of the local maritime captains wishing to stay within his good graces. This concept was later continued with the town of Brewster constructing two courses at one site named "the captains," paying homage to the dedicated men of the sea.

His first major sea adventure confronted him while serving as captain of the *Titan*. The weight of his cargo, the condition of his vessel, and the anger of the stormy sea combined to compromise the *Titan*, springing irreversible leaks in the boat. Water was pouring in at an unacceptable level. Being over one thousand miles to the nearest port of Brazil, a life and death executive decision was needed by the twenty-four-year-old captain. The captain's legal responsibility is to keep both the ship and its content as secure as possible, yet his moral and ethical charge is to the safety and well-being of the crew and passengers. If the ship goes down, all men are lost. If he commanded to abandon the ship, both the ship and cargo are gone.

For one full week, the crew stayed by his side, attempting to slow down the rapid intake of the water. It seemed impossible to stay afloat the necessary distance to reach the nearest safe harbor. Divine providence finally intervened. The crew was eventually forced to scuttle and take leave of the *Titan*. While in their lifeboat still distant from any form of solid land, the men were fortunately spotted by a passing Spanish brig and brought to safety.

He continued his sea voyages for eight more years before turning inland in 1861. His new career was as an entrepreneur, attempting to command the seas once more but this time externally from a desk. He formed the J. H. Sears Shipping Company, operating out of the port of Boston. This firm would have thirty-seven ships transporting all types of cargo worldwide. His company would become one of the largest in the United States. His roster of forty sea captains was unmatched anywhere you might search for captains on the Atlantic or Pacific coast. The combination of selecting excellent young sea captains, knowing every ship's structure and unique facets, and seeing what traded commodities were in high demand provided the vision for him to be an outstanding success in merchant marine ventures.

He was a founding member of the Pilgrim Club. Many acts of generosity and public benefit were performed by this group. The Club would later merge with the Cape Cod Memorial Association securing the necessary funds to build the Provincetown Monument. Most local sea captains were very proud of their *Mayflower* lineage and the Cape's history and traditions.

With his vast knowledge of ships, the sea itself, and the individual skill of the sea captains, he agreed to author "The Brewster Shipmasters." His book remains a valuable tool for maritime research. He retired in 1898, living to see President Theodore Roosevelt lay the cornerstone for Pilgrim's Monument in Provincetown and then invited President Taft to its inauguration.

The Pilgrims' Monument in Provincetown, Massachusetts. (Photo by Peter Whitlock)

Chatham

Origin of the Town's Name

The Native American tribe that lived in this area of the Cape before European colonization called themselves the Monomoynicks. Hence the region became known as Monomoit. Explorer Samuel de Champlain embarked here in October 1606, naming the area "Port Fortuné." As a result of an ownership dispute over a weapon, Champlain's men skirmished with the local indigenous people, eventually declaring it an unfit place to settle. Twelve years later, another group of Europeans arrived to apply the name of "Sutcliffe's Inlets."

Neither name became popular. Europeans did not permanently occupy the location until English settlers reached Monomoit in 1664. The town was incorporated on June 11, 1712, at which point it was renamed Chatham in honor of the Chatham Royal Navy Dockyards in county Kent, England. It is believed that the formation of Chatham's natural harbor closely resembled the shape of the Kent naval station.

A Brief History

William Nickerson chafed at the structure of the Crown Colony and the Church of England.

For that reason, he came to Monomoit (present-day Chatham) and made a deal for four square miles of land with the Monomoynick Sachem Mattaquason. However, this land was never officially registered with the official approval of the Plymouth Colony. The land dispute continued for sixteen years, eventually requiring William to pay a ninety pounds fee and secure a written deed from the sachem.

In 1802, Provincetown had 30 shipping vessels for cod and herring. Wellfleet had a goodly fleet for Mackerel and the oyster trade. Chatham went from 30 fishing boats in the 1780s down to only five fishing ships due to the impact of the revolutionary war.

Notable Connection to the Sea

In the town's early days, "mooncussers" would become a common sight in Chatham along the Monomoy Coast. On a moonless night, nefarious local shore dwellers would intentionally shine a bright light into the darkness to attract ships, challenging them to approach the uneven sandy shoals. These false lights became known as "Judas lights" as they exhibited treachery.

There was even a hill in the town nicknamed "Wicked Hill" to mark the spot of their evil deeds. Even the poet, Rudyard Kipling, heard of these actions and warned within his poem: "Ye mooncussers of Chatham, beware." In the early 1800s, there was an average of two shipwrecks every month. To counteract the deception and to protect against the dangerous shoals from Monomoy, Congress approved the construction of a twin-light lighthouse to be constructed in Chatham.

The station was established in 1808 by President Jefferson. It would become the second light station on Cape Cod. Second only to Highland Lighthouse, which went into service in 1797.

JOSEPH DOANE (1744–1801)
Mysterious Murders Committed at Sea

His fame grew louder with two very specific adventures in the sea. One as his connections was a mysterious maritime murder trial, and another was his role in the Revolutionary War at Stage Harbor.

In 1772, Captain Doane spotted a schooner flying distress signals. Coming alongside, he discovered the schooner *Abigail* in complete disarray. Captain Thomas Nickerson's body was on deck smeared with blood. The cousin of Captain Nickerson, Sparrow Nickerson, and his brother-in-law, Elisha Newcomb, also lay murdered on the top deck. Chests were smashed open. A barrel of rum stood on edge and was emptied of its contents. There was only one man left alive on the ship, Ansel Nickerson.

Doane approached Ansel Nickerson and listened to his story. As the only man left alive aboard the schooner, his story could not be corroborated. Doane brought Nickerson to dock to be formally held as a witness to the events. He presented a story that a pirate crew gained access to his boat, murdering all aboard. Seeing their arrival, he alone was able to lower himself to a dinghy, hiding below deck out of sight. After the pirates drank the rum and seized their booty, he claimed that they murdered all except for a fourteen-year-old cabin boy who they seized as a prisoner.

The story sounded plausible to Captain Doane, who related the full incident to the governor and Squire Bacon of the Barnstable court. Attorney Bacon was not satisfied with what information he could glean. More evidence was needed to form an opinion. Two frigates scoured the area for several days to see any signs of pirate activity in the immediate area. Not finding any proof, Ansell Nickerson was kept in jail on charges of murder on the high seas.

The trial lasted for two weeks and became a popular talking point within the early colonies. Future president John Adams and revolutionary patriot Josiah Quincy were counsel for the defense. Although he was eventually acquitted of all charges due to lack of evidence, there was then and is still now much doubt as to his complete innocence, over two centuries later.

Captain Doane later played a major role in the Battle of Stage Harbor. In 1782, a British privateer brazenly sought entrance to Chatham harbor to secure provisions from any ship that lay in anchor. A brigantine named the *Joseph* was in the harbor as its crew slept onshore. The privateers intended to seize control of that boat and an adjacent schooner.

A warning cannon exploded, alerting the locals that ships were being seized. Captain Doane and Colonel Benjamin Godfrey sprang into action. The ensuing volleys of muskets and arms must have impacted the fleeing vessels causing the *Joseph* to list on a sandbar. Once immobile, the local militia boarded the ship and reclaimed the American prize. The sloop was also chased down by boat and brought back to the harbor.

On that same day, Doane's sailors seized another British privateer. Before the war, Chatham could boast of thirty vessels and two hundred sailors. After the war, only five ships remained with a smattering of able-bodied seamen. Upon leaving military life, Doane served as a state representative from 1798 to 1790.

JOSHUA ATKINS (1777–1844)
The Twice Impressed Sea Captain

A descendent of British nobility, his lineage could be directly connected to Sir Robert Atkins, a Baron of the Exchequer to Charles I. His great grandmother, Constance Hopkins, bestowed him with Pilgrim heritage on his mother's side. These divided national loyalties were not uncommon in the very early days of a budding nation.

His first love was the sea. He took to it as a bird takes to the air. Following the ocean, he progressed to Captain of the 147-ton brig *Sally* by twenty-two. Three years after this promotion, he discovered his second love, Mehitable "Hittie" Eldredge. His third love was for the town of Chatham.

His desire to build a house had him sailing to Maine in 1799, where he undertook a mission to secure correctly sized lumber for its construction. Cape Cod, at this time, was devoid of large pieces of wood. Often the thin scrub pines would never suffice for building. Any decent-sized local lumber was used instead for building "try stations" (whale blubber burning stations) or saltworks.

Records indicate that in 1801, he had command of the schooner, the *Cameron*. A journal log specifies that an incredible time of twenty-five days was used to sail from Portugal to Boston. Any American sailing to the Atlantic ports of Europe in that era was fraught with danger. British control of the seas threatened the very safety of the crew and the loss of any vessel. Impressment into the British Royal Navy was a typical punishment and a ship seizure.

On three different occasions, he was captured by superior British maritime forces. On two of the occasions, complete forfeiture of the ship and its cargo was exacted. His loyalty to the new nation was never a question as he always refused to sail under the Union Jack. He avoided prison on each capture, most likely because of cargo forfeiture. Learning to outrun or avoid an enemy blockade became a useful naval skill to acquire.

As captain of the ship, the *Morning Star*, a final story of his bravery unfolded. Upon returning to the Cape from the West Indies, his ship neared Nantucket waters when privateers flying the British flag boarded. He did have some profits from his business venture on board but kept them well hidden.

There are two different versions of how the story continues. In one description, he was lashed to a cannon and was threatened with loss of life unless he revealed where the funds might be. He bravely defied this order numerous times. In another account, his pirate adversary noticed the markings of the Mason society on his clothes, of which he too was a member. They spared his life. Taking pity on him and recognizing his valiant efforts, his own life and crew were pardoned by his heroism. Despite all his efforts, his entire ship with all its content was eventually appropriated, never to be recovered.

Coming home alive and unharmed was greatly hailed as a victory by his wife Hattie and the town of Chatham. He sailed until 1827 and later transferred his maritime skills to the fishing and salt production industry.

JOSIAH HARDY (1822–1902)
The Longest Keeper of the Chatham Lighthouse

As was typical of many sea-loving men of this day, he first had a taste of ocean life by preparing fish and food for crewmen as a cook at the age of nine. His skills must have been acceptable as he kept his position for many years. His first ship master appointment was on the *Chatham* as appropriate to his passion and birthplace. The family name of Hardy was a very familiar occurrence for Chatham locals for over five generations.

Most of the ships he would command were owned by his cousin, Alpheus Hardy. To cite just a partial list of the ship names, three will be reported, the *Mountain Wave*, *Radiant*, and *Ocean Pearl.* Like his familial counterparts, his ships were deemed remarkable for their speed. In 1855, he traveled from Africa to Boston in twenty days which was a record for that period. He also loaded and returned transatlantic cargo on this same trip in an exceptional record of under two months.

There are many noted exploits of his sailing adventures. While loading a cargo of tea and clothes at Shanghai, he demonstrated clemency to two Mandarin citizens who were in search of political safety. He not only took them on board, but he also extended quite comfortable stateroom accommodations to them. As a small token of appreciation, a gift of carefully hand-carved teak picture frames was given to him, remaining a valuable family heirloom within his home to be passed on through the family for ages.

He arrived in China, Australia, Britain, Columbia, and the Philippines in one five-year ocean excursion. He was said to be the first captain to bring sugar to New York City from the Philippines on this voyage.

He was a successful businessman. Concurrent to claiming a partial shareholder of ten ships, he operated a very popular general store on Water Street. In 1871, he took his last transatlantic voyage on *the Ocean Pearl*, a 770-ton clipper, venturing from Spain to Boston. Unfortunately, this trip did not end well, with a storm causing a shipwreck of monumental proportions. His psychological and financial loss was only exacerbated when his store was also lost to erosion. By good fortune, his knowledge of the shipping industry would be an invaluable commodity for the next stage of his career as the keeper of the Chatham Light.

In 1872, he was appointed the Chatham Lighthouse Assistant for one year, followed by a permanent appointment later. By 1877, the previous twin wooden lighthouses were precariously close to the ocean's edge. It was determined that a new brick structure would be more suitable. The twin lenses were also transferred for the first time from burning lard oil to fixtures designed for kerosene. In 1881, the captain, now living in the new structure, witnessed the swallowing of the older structures and wharves built into the sea.

Being appointed a lighthouse keeper was a distinct honor for any well-connected political figure and a good financial decision. Due to poor health, he finally retired in 1890, remaining active in town affairs.

Old twin brick lighthouse of Chatham in 1844. (Provided by US Coastguard files.)

DAVID CROWELL (1820–1920)
Civil War Hero, and Chatham School Superintendent

At the first stage of his career, he engaged in the San Francisco gold rush days of 1849, transporting fortune seekers to the west coast. Men seeking a quick fortune felt that arriving in California would be their ticket to a new life. Posters of ships heading to the West Coast hinted of veins of gold nuggets yet to be discovered.

Several Chatham families pooled their funds to sponsor these gold rush adventures. David Crowell became a leader of this movement. Not only did he put up sizeable funds himself, but he also captained the boat, staying for a while in California so that the men's needs could be established. He opened a general merchant shop there and bakery, charging fairly high prices to keep his enterprise viable commercially.

In 1851, he once again, under the command of the *J.J. Cobb*, brought prospectors of gold mines bound to California. The men brought their wives and children this time, which expanded the California population considerably. He also stopped at Callao, Peru, to carry guano to Baltimore on his return trip. Then traded additional cargo back to Boston. Unfortunately, the overall local financial support for the Gold Rush eventually vanished, and the business failed, leaving the captain with accrued debt.

After serving on the sea for many years, in 1861, at forty-one years of age, he volunteered to be commissioned as a Master in the US Navy aboard the *Tuscarora*. He reported for duty in the Brooklyn Navy Yard, where American ships were docked. He reported to the commodore, eager to defend the Union cause. Working under the direction of Captain Craven, his first set of orders as a mate was to capture or sink the Confederate cruiser CSS *Nashville*. England heavily favored the Confederates, and there was conjecture that the English navy might enter the war as their ally. Later that month, *Tuscarora* sailed for Southampton, England, to complete their mission. CSS *Nashville* had encountered a Union blockade on 21 October, after crossing the Atlantic, becoming the first vessel to fly the Confederate flag in English waters.

She finally weighed anchor and departed on 3 February 1862, but *Tuscarora* could not pursue her as English law required that two enemy vessels could not leave port separated by less than 24 hours. This

The USS Tuscarora *in 1861. (Provided by US Navy files.)*

regulation infuriated the captain and his mate. One of the tactics used by the confederacy navy during the war was to utilize a higher range of technology despite being undermanned. Their ships were fewer but held more sophisticated maritime gear.

Captain and mate eventually took over the *Tuscarora* to serve as blockade duty off the coast for the US capital. Crowell remained active navy for a while longer until his health deteriorated, forcing his reluctant retirement before the end of the war. Upon his retirement from sea, he became Chatham's Superintendent of Schools and was credited with improving the school system. Near the end of his career, he was appointed the Chatham postmaster in 1903.

DAVID SMITH (1824–1886)
Entrepreneur in the Frozen Fish Process

David grew up in Chatham. His father, Stephen Smith, a successful local farmer, often heard his son express his wish to dedicate his life to seafaring journeys. He asked a friend to take David aboard a vessel on a long voyage and not be afraid to show him the grimly dark work in sailing. This mission was accomplished, but his passion for sailing only grew even stronger rather than being a deterrent.

In 1844, his first commission was as a full mate aboard the schooner *J. and L. Erickson*. His initial trips were coastal adventures, making loops between Boston and other East Coast ports such as Philadelphia and Charlestown. Once he received a more extensive taste of ocean life, he was fully hooked. He realized that the best way to earn a larger reward was to become a shipowner. He was determined to build a bark named the *Maria J. Smith* in honor of his second wife.

His skills as a general carpenter allowed him another source to earn funds. Still, another income was gained as a fish vendor utilizing enclosed seafood cans. The store became known as Smith and Armstrong, located on Old Wharf Road in Chatham.

Indications of his financial acuity are seen as he negotiated the sale of his canned fish business. He sold the rights of the fish packing commodities to Asa Nye in 1857. He then sold the building to his father. He attempted a whaling excursion for a short period, going to the Bering Straits and the Arctic Ocean but never felt the deep passion that emerged for him with transatlantic commercial trips.

On a trip to Havana, he noted that Spanish authorities deemed his American ship a deeply appreciated vessel. Rather than provoking violence or possible conflict, the ship was sold to Spanish officials at a healthy profit. He and his crew returned home safely on an American packet. He continued to work for several years, raising funds for his dreamed-upon boat. In 1862, his dream materialized. A boatyard in Portsmouth, New Hampshire, was commissioned to do the work for twenty-one thousand dollars. His specifications included that the afterdeck is made of hardwood, and living accommodations were placed on deck for his family and crew.

This ship served him well. His debts were paid in two years, and a handsome profit was realized. In 1864, he asked his wife to accompany him bound for Burma. Unfortunately, she had contracted cholera, dying on board. His grief was only intensified with the knowledge that if ice was readily available, her life might have been spared. Recognizing the financial, physical, and medical value that ice played on long sea voyages, his attention turned to its production. He first studied the designs of other ice storage systems and then perfected a prototype that was patented under his name. From 1871 to 1875, he stayed in Hawaii, perfecting his product.

Sailing card for the ship Maria J. Smith. *(Wilson and Company Printer.)*

This new design and fish production process proved to be a tremendous and popular boon for shipping. Within months, he established production and production centers in Cuba, Hawaii, California, and many Southern states. His product line became so in demand that the Smith Transparent Ice Company would establish a headquarter in Georgetown, Washington D.C., shipping ice worldwide. A process that congealed a mixture of ammonia and other products could be confined in a box and then shipped to distant ports

The business flourished, with many of his family members serving in key capacities. He eventually relocated to Washington but kept a firm relationship with his family in Chatham. At the time of his passing, he was overseeing the construction of the largest ice-making plants in the world in New Orleans. He died noted as being among the wealthiest men within the country.

Dennis

Origin of the Town's Name

The town was named after an early resident minister, Rev. Josiah Dennis. Not too much is known about the cleric. We know he was originally born on the North Shore of Massachusetts and graduated from Harvard. After his ordination, he accepted the position of the original ministry for the Second Parish of Yarmouth on June 22, 1727. His first wife, Bathsheba, died at an early age in 1745. He remarried Phoebe, with whom he had nine children. His parishioners viewed him as a clergyman with sincere piety. He possessed the attributes of earnest kindness, displayed heartfelt concern for the less fortunate, dedication to a reflective life, and consistently demonstrated a wry sense of humor that he often infused into his weekly sermons.

A Brief History

Dennis was first settled in 1639, by John Crowe (later spelled Crowell), Antony Thatcher, and Thomas Howes, as part of the town of Yarmouth. It was known then as the East Precinct. The original inhabitants who preceded English settlers called the northern sections of town Nobscusset, Sesuit, and Quivet. The town officially separated and incorporated in 1793. There was insufficient land for farming, so seafaring became one of the town's major industries in its early history, centering around the Shiverick Shipyard.

Six hundred sea captains made their homes in the small town of Dennis from the 1600s to the early 1900s. South Dennis had the most sea captains. Houses in the early 1800s may have had sufficient acreage to plant many crops, but the fragile soil was not fully conducive for farming. Nonetheless, many homes bore large families, some with four or five sons. These men sought life on the sea. Once a captain returned to Dennis describing his adventures and the exotic ports explored, the taste for adventure would endure for several generations.

Notable Connection to the Sea

In 1814, businessmen embarked upon establishing a harbor at Nobscusset. The Nobscusset Point Pier Company was officially commissioned through the Massachusetts legislature. Captains included Daniel Howes Zena Howes, Henry Hall, John Howes, and Oren Howes. Most of these men were either neighbors, friends, or relatives of each other. In most cases, families would see their children intermarry as well.

When completed, the Nobscusset wharf became the landing place for packet boats going to and from Boston. Greater demand ensued, and the town's most famous commercial enterprise, the shipyard at Sesuit Harbor, came to be. Asa Shiverick (1790–1861), a master shipbuilder, established the shipyard. He turned out sloops, schooners, brigs, and ships for over two generations, equal in beauty and size to any ship in New England. As the shipyard gained experience in their craft, they moved from sloops and schooners to produce eight merchant vessels of extreme grace and majesty that would rival any ship made in America.

Captains lived in every part of Dennis. East Denis has its captain Crowells, Howes, Sears, and Halls. Dennisport had its Wixons and Kelleyes. Dennis Center had more Howes, Halls, and Crowells, while South Dennis could claim Thatchers, Kelleyes, Nickersons, and Baxters. West Dennis accounted for the most sea captains with names such as Studies, Kelleyes, Crowells, Bakers, and Baxters. In all, some four hundred Dennis seamen achieved the rank of captain. In 1837, there were 150 registered masters of sea vessels belonging to the town of Dennis sailing to various ports around the world.

CAPTAIN DANIEL HOWES (1795–1875)
Inspiration Behind Corporation Pier

The Howes family, Captain Ebenezer Howes, his nephew Prince Howes and his cousin Jonathan Howes were all Dennis residents that owned "try works "on their local property. A try works contained a huge furnace designed to turn whale blubber into various oils and refined substances. Before whaling became a major industry in New Bedford, local smaller boats would secure a whale, dragging it to the shore, then the entire carcass was brought in for processing. The Howes family quickly realized that dragging whales to shore in the early 1700s was unwieldy and not very efficient. They suggested it would be more productive to install a furnace directly on a deck to facilitate the processing of blubber making allowing for longer periods at sea.

Captain Daniel Howes recorded his profession as a "sailing foreigner," indicating his maritime journeys took him across oceans. Relatives of this captain have letters he wrote from the ports of Portugal, Spain, and Russia as he carried goods on his schooner, *Harriet*. After a long, lucrative career, he retired in Dennis at his home in Nobscusset Point. He played a major role in the establishment of the corporation. He eagerly supported the idea of financing a large pier in Dennis, which would become a window to the world. The fishermen of North Dennis now had a deep harbor from which they could sail.

The Shivrick Boatyard, artist rendering. (Courtesy of the Dennis Historical Society.)

To finance the pier, thirty shares were sold to a total of fourteen stockholders, mostly in the Halls and Howes family. A wharf of stone and wood was first created at the easterly side of Nobscussset Point, running for six hundred feet. When completed, the local citizenry referred to it as Corporation Road, and the area is still called Corporation Beach today. As the pier became more utilized, demand increased as packets boats to Boston were a boon to the local town's economy. With more ships in the region, the demand to add to a fleet also increased, thus creating the opportunity for the town's most famous commercial enterprise, the shipyard at Sesuit Harbor.

CAPTAIN HENRY HALL (1761–1850)
Redefined the Growing of Cranberry on The Cape

Records indicate Captain Hall fought in the American Revolution. After his sailing days, he turned inland to make a living. In 1816, Hall began by fencing in a field of wild cranberries to protect the fruit from animals. When the plants thrived, he transplanted them to his cranberry yards. In 1820 Hall produced 30 barrels of cranberries, which he shipped to New York for sale. He is credited as the first large producer of the cranberry crop.

Cranberries were a natural growing fruit on Cape Cod. For over ten thousand years, the Wampanoag people have enjoyed their annual harvest known as "sasumuneash." As the glaciers receded, the lower plots of land produced vines in the newly formed kettle ponds. The combination of sand, clay, and debris were perfect natural elements to start the growth of a tart-flavored fruit. As his property was near the coast, he frequently tracked the weather's effects on his crops. His observation was that the flooding of water over the sandy surface would protect the plant from insects and ice and become an easier process for final gathering.

He further noticed that wild cranberries grew faster and stronger when sand grew over them in his bog. When his neighboring farmers learned of his creative techniques, he became their instructor and consulted with many farmers starting an industry that would thrive for more than two centuries.

Although some agricultural purists were at first offended by the idea, the concept of adding sand eventually became an accepted process. Many

Cranberry picking on Cape Cod postcard promotion.

Cape Cod farmers now intentionally converted their swamp, wetlands, peat bogs, and wet meadows into cranberry bogs.

Eventually, the crop became so plentiful on the Cape that demand for additional workers would entice Finnish and Cape Verdeans immigrants who started to arrive at Cape Cod to toil in the emerging agriculture trade.

CAPTAIN JOSHUA SEARS (1817–1885)
A Most Meticulous Sailor

Joshua was born in 1817. At ten years of age, he chose a profession of which he was both passionate and proved to be well suited. He was the first mate at the age of twenty-three, and at thirty, in 1847, was in command of the *Burmah,* his first ship. His personal goal was to command only the finest of ships.

His scrupulous neatness on board and conscientious preservation of any property entrusted to his care were well known, enabling him to choose any vessel he preferred from a fleet. His crew was aware of his particular attention to order and civility. Any misbehavior such as excessive drinking, vulgar language, or mishandling the piety of the Sabbath day would never be tolerated. He preferred trips requiring deep-sea voyages, visiting the East Indies nineteen times, and often touching upon China and the Sandwich Islands.

His experience of forty years on the sea was seen as more extensive and more responsible to its cargo than most of his contemporaries. His logbooks describing many long voyages were filled with significant perilous events. His attentive command assured his financial supporters that his freight would never suffer accident or loss. On the 11th of June 1840, he was married to Minerva, daughter of William & Sally (Small) Handren of Harwich.

His wife accompanied the captain on four long voyages, the last being on the *Wild Hunter,* circumnavigating the world. He left the sea during the War of the Rebellion, retiring to a modest home in East Dennis, where he died on the 22 of March 1885. He was much beloved by the entire community for his genial, uniformly kind, and upright character and the shipowners and the commercial world for his fine, just, and reliable dealings.

His record is of honor, honest labor, and well-executed duties. He was a model seaman and officer and a humble man who could preserve old friendships and make other people happy by examples of his kind and generous spirit.

He came to command the ship, *Wild Hunter*, which was the pride of the Shivrick clippers. His ship logs and letters reveal an articulate world traveler with a wonderful human side in his stern New England exterior. You can read his resolute trepidations in his 1857 log entry, "The heavy swell keeps running from the west. Patience, Patience—place your trust in God." Further on, he wrote: "Oh how disconsolate, I do feel. Next voyage, I will go down to the China Sea and face all the typhoons that blow."

His written letters reflect a man who enjoyed the company of his wife. "To facilitate the enthusiasm of Minerva, I encouraged her guardianship of many species of animals such as goats, pigs, and birds, both to keep her amused and to add to the livestock of home." Minerva was distinguished as an entertainer who frequently welcomed the captain of any passing ship to dine onboard while preparing a sumptuous repast. Her musical skills would assuredly become the focus of many a gala party.

He spent over three years, from 1857 to 1860, afloat. The *Wild Hunter* traveled from Boston to San Francisco, then across the pacific to Singapore during his final voyage. He mentioned the acquisition of lumber, clothing, and machinery such as a turning lathe as he traversed the pacific. His fondness for cats was evident as he cited his admiration of their grace and speed. His last twenty-five years were spent in Dennis, where he was an esteemed member of the community elected to serve in several voluntary posts.

CAPTAIN PRINCE CROWELL (1846–1918)
A Protector of African Slaves

His was a Quaker family, and as a youth, Prince Sears attended the Quaker Seminary on Spring Hill in Sandwich, Massachusetts. When he became old enough to go to sea, Prince served as a purveyor of cargo on sailing vessels his father captained. Given the title of "supercargo collector," Prince oversaw the buying and selling all the ship's cargo. Prince eventually became a captain himself of various vessels trading up and down the coast of the United States and to England and Europe. His experience had taught him how to trade merchandise in many foreign ports. His initial cargo load from his ships would often be cotton from the southern United States, which was in high demand.

Captain Crowell became bothered by the concept of transporting and trading cotton based on the cruel labor of slaves. Because of his Quaker upbringing, he was adamantly against all forms of slavery. He would become an ardent abolitionist. When his shipping business took him to New Orleans, he was in mortal danger since he was an admitted contributor and subscriber to the *Liberator*, a well-known antislavery magazine, and his many acquaintances of professed abolitionists. His life was frequently imperiled with bodily harm.

When Methodism swept Cape Cod, the Captain's family joined the Red Top Methodist Church in Brewster. However, when they found this church was not fully abolitionist, they left the Red Top Church to establish their church in East Dennis. While the members of this church were against slavery, they once decided not to allow a former slave to come to speak to the congregation. The Captain, who did not agree with this decision, became upset and decided to take his pew out of the church.

At thirty-three, Captain Crowell made a trading trip to the Far East. He left in February of 1846 and returned the following October. Raisins, tobacco, and fish were some of the goods in his cargo. This was a very successful trip for the captain. He did not go to sea again, but he continued his association with shipping by holding shares in or becoming the sole owner of many vessels. He also became one of the backers of the Shiverick Boatyard in Dennis.

By the mid-19th century, many Cape Cod seamen, including Captain Crowell, were incensed by the Fugitive Slave Law of 1850, demanding runaway slaves be returned to their masters. He saw the regulation as being excessively malicious. On Sept. 22, 1860, the Cape Cod Anti-Slavery Convention was held. He met with the assembled in Harwich Exchange Hall, insisting upon "Immediate and Unconditional Abolition." Many of his friends had homes with trapdoors, fake walls, and underground tunnels giving rise to the speculation of an underground railroad system at Cape Cod.

After leaving the sea, the captain was involved in many ventures outside the shipping business. He started the first major salt works in Boston. He was part owner and first president of the Pacific Guano Factory in Woods Hole, Massachusetts. He was instrumental in starting the Old Colony Railroad. This railroad was needed to service the guano factory in Woods Hole, of which the captain was now part-owner and president. He later became President of the Bank of Cape Cod, elevating it to one of the successful financial ventures in the region.

CAPTAIN MARCUS LAFAYETTE HOWES (1858–1902)
A Celebrated Colonial Murder Trial

According to The Japanese Weekly newspaper of October 13, 1888, the Boston District Court related data on the trial of Captain Marcus Howe. Captain Howes was a Dennis resident who would make frequent trips carrying cargo from Boston to Japan. On one occasion, he was aboard the bark, the *Freeman,* crossing the Atlantic from New York to Tokyo.

Based on verbal challenges with his first mate and crew, our captain felt compelled to quickly replace his current crew with a rapidly selected new group of seamen. Hence, fourteen new Japanese sailors were recruited for their return voyage. Only the Japanese mate spoke English, so the orders were always relayed in translation to the full crew through this mate. He could not find a suitable first mate but could find a German sailor as his second mate. His eleven-ton bark was hauling kerosene oil as its major cargo.

A significant challenge arose while the voyage to Japan followed the usual trade route from Java, Europe via the Cape of Good Hope, and then back home to Boston. One of the Japanese sailors, Hidaku Kikumatsu, was particularly recalcitrant. His verbal arguments with the crew were loud and vociferous. At one point, he even threatened to throw the first mate overboard.

While the vessel was traveling from the coast of Java, Kikumatsu's rants intensified. Having a very sick man on board, the captain personally washed him, hoping to prevent infection. Kikumatsu did not see the efficacy of cleaning. He suggested to the ill mariner that the washing stop. Not knowing what was said, the captain asked for a translation to find out that he was being criticized.

The captain summoned Kikumatsu to him, who ran into the forecastle. Capt. Howes demanded the sailor to surrender, but instead, there was a claim that the sailor sprang forward with a knife in his hand. In the ensuing scuffle, Capt. Howes shot him, and the Japanese sailor subsequently died. The rest of the voyage proceeded uneventfully, and upon return to the United States, Capt Howes filed a full report of the incident.

A major maritime trial occurred in 1888. Capt. Howes believed that he acted in self-defense to protect his crew and vessel. During his trial, the crew's testimony was given in Japanese and was translated for the jurors. The American steward testified that Kikumatsu threatened Capt. Howes. Every member of the Japanese crew testified that the killing was unwarranted.

Nevertheless, the jury found Capt. Howes guilty and sentenced him to three years at Barnstable House of Correction. Judge Grey made two interesting points on the case. First, he believed that the significance of an oath might be different for Buddhists than it might be for Christians. The judge also noted that the relevancy of the concept of perjury might be different for the two religious groups.

The captain appealed the final verdict, eventually leading to a pardon granted by President Benjamin Harrison. Nonetheless, the trial had a chilling impact on future ship masters. In dealing with a mutinous crew, a captain must mete out negative sanctions both swiftly and with judicious considerations The local friends of Capt. Marcus consistently displayed their full support for him. The captain eventually retired to Dennis, spending his final days as an accepted and esteemed citizen of the community.

President Benjamin Harrison. (Permission by the US Bureau of Engraving and Printing.)

Eastham

Origin of the Town's Name

The name Eastham has two possible derivations. It is most likely selected as an honor paid to the English town of Eastham in Cheshire. An original settler, John Doane, came from East Ham, a suburb of London in Essex County.

The other but much more unlikely option is just the fact that it is a village in the "east end" of Cape Cod. "Ham" is a typical English ending assigned to a local village. Originally the area was known as "Nauset" by the early settlers, as called by the residency of the indigenous people. It extended to the west to the Yarmouth border and south to Orleans.

A Brief History

A salient fact to consider is that Eastham was the only town on Cape Cod founded by Pilgrims. It was originally home to the Nauset people. Things rapidly changed in 1643. A group of Pilgrims dissatisfied with the barren soil and small allotment of land ceded to them by the Puritan hierarchy set out in a different direction. The Plymouth church sent out a committee to examine the Nauset Indian Territory. Seven members of the group decided to stay: Edward Bangs, Josias Cook, John Doane, Richard Higgins, Thomas Prence, John Smalley, and Nicholas Snow. They were impressed by the coastal waters and abundance of trees in the area.

In 1644, these "newcomers" (all having come to the new land on either the "Mayflower," the "Fortune," or the "Ann") brought their families to Nauset. There was a total of forty-nine people in all. Some years later, the town was officially incorporated, with the name changing to Eastham in 1651.

One of the very earliest industries in Eastham was shipbuilding. One of the town's founders, Edward Bangs, was recorded in 1641 as having "superintended" the very first ship in the Plymouth Colony, a bark between forty and fifty tons. It is more than likely that some of the earliest settlers of Eastham traveled across the bay in a ship constructed by Edward Bangs.

Stranded whales were a common sight in Eastham. It was the custom to have a town-wide signal pop up whenever a whale was sighted. Th townspeople would set out in small boats to claim a portion of the whale. An early Eastham minister, Deacon John Paine, was once in the middle of a sermon when he heard that a beached whale was detected offshore. He abruptly ended his sermon, yelling out, "Now start fair," as he too scrambled to claim his portion of blubber. It became so competitive that the town decided to divide the towns into specific geographic sections that could claim their degree of wealth from the sea in rotation.

Eastham never became a comprehensive fishing port like many other cape towns despite having a large natural harbor. Nonetheless, most sea-faring men were engaged in the merchant service sailing from Boston to coastal ports or the West Indies. Although the harbor was never widened, some large ships could enter a channel between Nauset Beach and Nauset Heights. For example, a large two-mast schooner named the *Nettie M. Rogers* regularly sailed down the cove in the second half of the 1800s, carrying a cargo of coal, lumber, and grain.

Notable Connection to the Sea

Oddly enough, one of its strongest relationships to the sea emerged with a 1954 National Park Service study. It was determined that only 240 miles of coastal land throughout the entire country was available to state or federal authorities for public recreation. This report originally identified sixteen potential priority areas to acquire. The Great Beach on the Outer Cape, with its long unbroken miles of undeveloped seashore property, jumped out as perhaps the best option.

In 1961, when John F. Kennedy was President and Tip O' Neil was the Speaker of the House, two men who had both owned summer homes at the Cape talks progressed in earnest. On August 7, 1961, the establishment of the Cape Cod National Seashore became a reality. Today the Seashore encompasses more than 43,000 acres and attracts more than five million visitors each year. Upon signing the bill, Kennedy remarked 'Its goal is to preserve the natural and historic values of a portion of Cape Cod for the enjoyment of all people in the United States."

For the first time, the federal government would create a national park out of mostly privately owned land. Months of hearings and adjustments were needed to author a bill that balanced private and public interests. Within the park's confines, in an area called Fort Hill, stands the home of the Whaler John Penniman, recording the maritime heritage of park lands. A series of biking trails, nature walks, and beach pathways cross over the park extending from the tip of Provincetown down to almost the Orleans line.

JOSEPH ATWOOD (1720–1794)
Shrewd Captain who Sailed into Danger

Joseph was originally born an Eastham man but eventually settled and typically is more connected to Chatham. He entered the sea as a cook as a young boy. In the 1740s, sailors from the Monomoy Point region began to take longer and longer sea voyages using a "snow," pronounced "Snoo," which is a two-mast vessel designed to handle cargo efficiently. His snow *Judith* was a square sterned ship of 80 tons, compact in size and only able to support a small crew.

Atwood chose to attempt some of the more hazardous trips in his early sailing days, frequently venturing to the West Indies, which had become a bastion for rum runners, slave traders, and pirates. One of his original routes took him from the Bay of Honduras, then to venture off to Amsterdam and then return to New England.

In addition to mastering his snow, Atwood took command of the schooner, The *Isle Sables Gallery*. He used this vessel to sail to England and Amsterdam. A third vessel be commanded was the sloop *Falmouth*. Records indicate that while embarking on a venture in 1749, his cargo of high-grain excellent quality lumber from Nova Scotia brought him traveling across the Atlantic, bringing him record amounts of revenue for his company and himself.

It is evident that the financial sponsors of world trading were aware of the dangers that lurked on the seas but still expected their commanders of the sea to be courageous heroes. Before taking command of the ship *Judith,* the owners wrote to him, "While you are loading your ship in Honduras, you must keep a good lookout lest you will be overpowered by the Spaniards. You are well fitted for the defense, and we expect you to offer a manly defense in the event of an attack."

Being a man of cautious predisposition, Atwood would carefully prepare to dispatch his duty. The captain utilized the data of gathering naval intelligence to plan his voyages. He often secured data by bribing local sources to ascertain which Spanish ships might be in nearby Honduran waters and where exactly they were located. He moved about stealthily through the waters, quickly entering and leaving the port in the early morning hours.

His cargo mainly consisted of marine life caught when he traveled along the shores of Nova Scotia in the heart of the fishing industry. His log notes that in 1768 he transported white pine boards, white pine shingles, clapboards, and laths to Boston. His products from Amsterdam were most likely teas, fine wines, silk dresses, and fine dinnerware that suited the needs of his affluent customers.

The Atwood House. (Courtesy of the Chatham History Society.)

Commanding the schooner *Isle Sables Galley*, his entire crew would frequently be as small as six men with one first mate and the rest crew. His acquisition of wealth was sizable in pre-colonial America. He used his resources to purchase thirty acres in the vicinity of Stage Harbor in Chatham, where he built his dream mansion. In his retirement, he turned his interests to farming. He left livestock such as pigs, cows, and horses to his beloved wife, Deborah. Today, The Atwood Museum and House (Chatham Historical Society) stands on these very grounds.

CAPTAIN EDWARD PENNIMAN (1831–1913)
"A Whaler of Superior Skills"

Edward Penniman was born in Eastham in 1831. At the age of eleven, he was called to the sea, volunteering to be a cook on a schooner bound for the coast of Newfoundland. He continued working with several other fishing vessels along the coast. Eventually, the exciting lure of chasing "the largest mammal on earth," the immense proportionality of the whale beckoned. In his teens, he proceeded to the whaling center of New England located in New Bedford.

His very first whaling expedition was at the age of twenty-one. He served as a boat steerer. Being an able and quick student of ocean-related skills, he was a second mate for his second voyage and took command of the ship when called upon to do so.

His first three voyages aboard the *Minerva* between 1855 and 1868 launched his successful career. Two of these early trips were destined for the South Pacific, but the third took him to the artic. By the mid-1850s, the whaling process diminished greatly from the New England coast, taking adventurers more towards the Artic Ocean. By this point, whaling became a more complex endeavor with larger ships installed with large steel "trys" (boiling cauldrons) and blubber racks.

These trips were followed with the vessel *Cicero* going to the artic from 1874 to 1875; the *Europa* from 1876 to 1879, journeying to Patagonia; and the *John A. Howland* going to the artic from 1881 to 1884. Gustie, his wife, would usually accompany him. It is said that his lifemate was a far cry from a traditional sea captain guest. She would often engage in strenuous labor and take control of many navigational functions. His children would also be aboard for the many years he spent at sea. Their "homeschooling" would also be far from a normal project for their typical education compared to their Cape Cod peers.

At one point, the captain, in a fit of poor judgment, felt that raising a polar bear cub would make a fine sport for his sons to enjoy. However, the cub had other ideas. At first, the bear howled through the darkness of the night and then eventually escaped from his pen. Once freed, the animal chased the sailors across the deck, showing the ferocity of even a young cub. The sailors climbed the rigging to avoid his fury. Finally, after the cub had his sport, he jumped overboard, swimming away to freedom.

On his whaling ship venture on the *Minerva*, he served as an auxiliary Union Naval officer. A Confederate charged vessel, named the *Shenandoah*, was known to be in search of whalers and, in particular, his very ship. Receiving a tip from a French captain that he was being hunted, he spotted the *Shenandoah* in the distance. Being equipped with a cannon was a most useful blessing. Penniman struck first, delivering a cannon ball blast to their deck, damaging the cabin. The *Shenandoah* limped away and was never seen again in this conflict.

During his 1879 voyage, he secured 1,200 barrels of sperm oil, 4,200 barrels of whale oil, and 20,000 pounds of whale bone, which was a tremendous haul for any whaler at any stage in this era. He purchased twelve acres of land at Fort Hill in Eastham. It was a most modern house for its day, being the first in town to have indoor plumbing. Today, this home is maintained through the efforts of the National Park Service, hosting thousands of annual guests who tour Cape Cod.

Gustie displayed her maritime skills on one voyage when her husband was on dryland seeking supplies while the ship was blown to the ocean by a rapidly arriving hurricane. With the assistance of only a skeleton crew, she was able to return the ship to port.

His voyage aboard *the Howland* would be his last. Upon returning to his ample farm in Eastham, he desired the sea no more. He would spend more than half of his natural life directly at sea but acquired great wealth in doing so. He had two cows, a flock of chickens, and a greenhouse to occupy his time. He also took an interest in local affairs, being among the founding members of the First Universalist Church in his hometown.

The Edward Penniman House in Eastham. (Courtesy of the National Park Service Archives)

CAPTAIN FREEMAN HATCH (1820–1889)
A Competitive Ship Racer

Freeman Hatch, the captain of the clipper *Northern Lights*, accomplished a feat of shipping history that is enshrined on his tombstone. Freeman Hatch "holds the record time for sailing from San Francisco to Boston." The inside story of this trip was associated with a wager. Hatch had a new clipper, confident his ship could defeat all competition. William Brewster, a famed shipmaster, also possessed a newly christened vessel. They both rounded Cape Horn on their 38th day out at sea. All were tied. Captain Hatch passed the *Boston Light* at 10 A.M. 1853 and sailed into Boston harbor. He has won his race by a span of over two days.

A Boston merchant joined the wagering competition. The merchant offered a brand-new suit for the captain to defeat two different vessels, one was named *the Trade Wind*, and the other was called appropriately enough the *Contest* on a return voyage to Boston. *The Trade Wind* left on March 10, and his *Northern Lights* left three days later. Captain Hatch felt confident that he could beat two New York-based vessels.

Early in the race, he passed *the Trade Wind* with ease. As he reached the Cape of Good Horn, the two ships were in direct sight of each other for several days. By the point of the equator, by hard driving, he pulled slightly ahead by forty miles or so. Far more beneficial to him was the wind factor regarding his geographic position. Being eastward of his adversary, he had a favorable wind, arriving in port a full two days before his nearest competitor. He traveled from Boston to San Francisco in the record time of seventy-six days and six hours, a tremendous record for this era.

Arriving in Boston, even before the counting-house was open, he traveled by carriage to Roxbury to meet the ship's owner, James Huckins. The owner was awoken from his sleep but was delighted for the inconvenience, rewarding him with an immense financial incentive for his victory.

Racing was in his blood. A mere four months later, seven clippers between August 4th and the 16th all set sail for the western coast. The owners held a regatta heading from Boston to San Francisco. The captain knew that his ship was seriously strained from its recent trip but did not wish to be left out of the competition. The challenge of this race was a dare he could not resist. The *Northern Lights, Trade Wind, Raven, Witch of the Wave, Hurricane, Comet,* and *Mandarin*, boasted of their quality construction and seaworthiness.

As the race consisted of a voyage of more than 15,000 miles, all seven vessels reached their destination harbor within six days. He was not quite as fortunate this time as he arrived in third place. His facial and verbal disappointment was evident for months afterward.

Captain Hatch's next command was the *Bonita,* another clipper ship owned and designed by Huckins. He now engaged in a two-year cruise. His first port of call was Batavia in the West Indies which he reached in seventy-seven days. From there, he was bound for le Havre, reaching it in eighty-three days. Then he shipped coal from Cardiff, which he transferred to Shanghai in seventy-eight days. His whirlwind trip continued as he was now bound for London. His long voyage ended as he brought iron to Calcutta, but the trip was never completed. His ship began leaking so badly that she needed to be condemned.

As a young mate from Eastham, he was known to have three beautiful sisters. The local people respected his ocean exploits to a phenomenal degree. Many believe the three lighthouses in Eastham were knick-named "The Three Sisters" as a tribute to his three attractive sisters. Upon retirement, he served in several official capacities for the town of Eastham. Specifically, he championed the improvement and construction of improved roads along the Route 6 corridor.

CAPTAIN HOPPY MAYO (Dates Uncertain)
War of 1812, the Captain Who Hid in Eastham

Cape Cod captains also played a major role in the War of 1812. Two of the Eastham captains, Mathew Hopkins (Hoppy) Mayo and Winslow Lewis Knowles, were frequent clipper runners taking products from the Cape to Boston and beyond. In July 1814, a smaller whaleboat was utilized so that the two captains could deliver a shipment of rye to the Boston Harbor.

With the British establishing a naval blockade of the Boston harbor, ships cautiously approached this brave endeavor. In fact, the contour of the Eastham coast and most of Cape Cod was subjected to the treachery imposed by the British ships lurking from the shores. As a result of this embargo, all commerce was either fully stopped or was condemned to become a potential prize of seizure.

The bravery of the local captains was noteworthy yet foolhardy. In truth, many of the British navigators were well-known within her majesty's navy. Just before the start of the new 1812 war, the two captains would often discuss the perils of the Cape shoals with the British. Alas, the pair of colonial captains were spotted attempting to sneak into port. At first, Knowles was released. Later a ransom demand was made for the secure return of Captain Mayo. British sailors took command of the vessel, seizing it as a prize of war.

Unwisely, the British also permitted Mayo to continue his voyage under their watchful eye. It was felt that his background with the dangers of the treacherous waters was best served with the most available help. However, this thinking would only backfire. Hoppy craftily brought them extremely close to a large shoal, suggesting the boat anchor for the night. When dawn broke, the ship was sitting on a strand of sand. Its proximity to the shore meant that Eastham militiamen could walk directly to the boat, seizing the British sailors as captives. The prisoners were then marched to the Crosby tavern in Eastham.

On the shore, George Collins, Obed Sparrow, Atty. Harding Knowles and blacksmith Peter Walker kept the prisoners in custody. These actions certainly caught the British off guard yet defiant. Having superior weapons and control of the sea, the British naval powers threatened to blast the town to unrecognizable lengths. The town needed to capitulate and finally did release their newly acquired captives.

By now, they were also keen at collecting a ransom of $1200 for the delivery of Captain Mayo. The ransom was paid, but American inventiveness saved the day once again. After the money was received, Captain Mayo knew of many hiding places and was acquainted with the whole town, who successfully granted him safe refuge in many secure places within the Eastham shores. The residents of Eastham spoke of him proudly showing his many hiding places to his own grandchildren years after the event passed.

CAPTAIN ISAAC FREEMAN (1733–1807)
A Patriot of the American Revolution

Captain Freeman was a distinguished and well-respected sea merchant from Eastham. During the American Revolution, his rank was posted as general seamen. He engaged in coastal shipping assignments, moving needed products away from prying British warships into safe ports to assist the American cause. His wife, Thankful, also came from a revered local maritime family, the Higgins

The Boston Maritime Society was first officially incorporated in 1754. The initial founders included William Starkey, Edward Cahill, Isaac Freeman, Richard Humphreys, Edward Freyer, Moses Bennet, Jonathan Clarke, John Cullum, Joseph Prince, and Abraham Remmick.

The Boston Maritime Society had a primary goal of improving navigation in and around Boston Harbor. John Foster Williams, a member of the Society, commanded America›s first revenue cutter, the predecessor to the Coast Guard, and took as his special task the drawing of an accurate chart for Cape Cod Bay. The construction of lighthouses and placement of buoys and markers has often been accomplished with the Society's advice. Of particular concern to the Society was the appointment of competent sailors new to the safe passages for vessels in and out of the port. Beginning in 1791 and continuing through the present day, the Society through its Trustees is vested with the authority to nominate Pilot Commissioners, who appoint Boston Harbor maritime pilots.

Among his six children, two of his sons Edmund Freeman, Senior and Benjamin Freeman, would continue in the family business of commercial shipping. He eventually moved to Wellfleet, where he generously served as a benefactor to widows who lost their men at sea. He is buried in Eastham, and his grave is appropriately marked as an American Revolutionary veteran.

The Nixes Mate, a navigational guide in Boston Harbor. (Boston Maritime Society Structure, by Eric Kilby, Sommerville Massachusetts.)

Falmouth

Origin of the Town's Name

Falmouth, England in Cornwall, was the initial port of departure for Bartholomew Gosnold when he sailed in 1602. Falmouth in England is where King Henry VIII built his castle in Pendennis to defend "where the creeks crossed." This local area of Cape Cod was historically called "Suckanesset" (land of black shells). It later became Falmouth when it was officially incorporated in 1686. Many of its various sections retain Wampanoag names such as Waquoit, Quisset, Sippewisset (small cove), and Megansett on the east. More inland, we see the villages of Teaticket (land of large rivers), Smalltown and Hatchville

A Brief History

Falmouth was first settled by English colonists four decades after the Mayflower landing. Due to its large natural deep-water harbor at Woods Hole, large sailing ships could easily access internal Falmouth enterprises. One of the first industries in the area was raising Marino sheep. Detailed records on sheep pastures on Naushon Island reveal that the territory was inundated with free-ranging sheep in 1679. About fifty sheep per square mile would become the norm. This seven-mile-long Elizabethan Island later becomes the summer retreat of the Forbes family. Later, larger merchant ships, built at the Shiverick boatyard, would sail worldwide carrying fertilizer and exotic foods to many foreign ports, all departing from Falmouth harbor.

Notable Connection to the Sea

Falmouth was the only Cape Cod town that witnessed naval activity during two wars. British soldiers would occasionally raid the sheep herds on Naushon Island during the Revolutionary War. The HMS *Faulklands* was docked within the cove. In one adventure of 1779, desperately needing more supplies, the British landed to secure livestock in Woods Hole from the farm of Ephraim Swift. Major Joseph Dimmick was appointed militia commander for the local area. He and his troops followed the British seamen. Just as they were about to slaughter the livestock, he pounced to chase the British back to their boat, forcing them to retreat in hunger.

Then in the War of 1812, British vessels returned to Falmouth. Two British ships entered Tarpaulin Cove early in the year 1814. Just as they did in the previous war, John Slocum warned the town of pending disaster. The HMS *Nimrod* fired at least two hundred and fifty cannon balls directly into the town. As the British shelled Falmouth, Ichabod Hatch sat defiantly on his front stoop. He wondered if they might be ever to do it again. Sure enough, a second cannonball whizzed right over his head. Remnants of cannon fire are still visible in several local homes and shops. One Falmouth resident, Elijah Swift, was so concerned when his home was damaged that he constructed a 50-ton schooner to prepare for battle, which he built in his front yard in one year.

A British privateer with an aptly named ship *Retaliation* also came to wreak havoc on the town. A very shrewd captain named Weston Jenkins stowed thirty-one men on his ship, the *Two Friends*. Feigning to be unarmed in a "Trojan Horse" type maneuver, he permitted the privateers to board his ship while the rest of the hidden sailors pounced from hiding to make their way onto the *Retaliation*, capturing it without one single shot being fired. Today, Woods Hole Oceanographic Institution (WHOI) is the world's leading independent non-profit organization dedicated to researching and exploring the ocean.

ASA SHIVERICK (1790–1861)
Established the Pacific Guano Company at Woods Hole

In the 1850s, the United States searched for an innovative material that could assist farming and move heavy machinery. Asa Shiverick found a way to help. Current farm applications of lime or crop rotation did little to rejuvenate the sandy soil. Sea captains on the western coast of South America stumbled upon a potential solution. Guano or hardened bird and bat excrement was in abundance in several islands, and when mixed with fish scrap and menhaden (small forage fish), the mixture was a perfect fertilizer for new plant life. In particular, the coast of Peru held an abundance of guano (bat or bird dung) that greatly enriched the soil.

The Pacific Guano Company was formed in 1859, rapidly becoming one of the region's largest employers. More than two hundred men, primarily Irish immigrants, were hired for work. The new Shiverick shipyards in Dennis made sturdy commercial ships capable of supplying fertilizer to farmers worldwide.

A perfect source of fertilizer was now established to meet growing demand. At one point, the Peruvian government increased their shipping costs to unreasonable heights to allow the cultivation of guano. In addition, many unscrupulous owners mistreated slave labor from China. In 1856, the United States government passed The Guano Act allowing American sailors to claim uninhabited islands as a personal possession with mining rights to secure this valuable commodity and protect against slavery.

A very devout abolitionist family named Crowell wished to invest in an emerging profitable trade, particularly when it might reduce Chinese slavery in Peru. It was noticed that many whalers were returning to Cape Cod from the coast of California either partially or fully devoid of product. So, the pre-existing Shiverick shipyard enterprise joined forces with the fortune of the Glidden and Williams family to establish the Pacific Guano Company. With governmental regulations and moral authority on their side, their company acquired the Howland Islands, 1800 miles southwest of Hawaii.

They had thirty-three ships in use at the beginning of their business, with only six being lost on their return voyage. Two of their original ships were later captured by Confederate forces. Its location at Woods Hole was appropriate for deep-sea journeys. Some of the Woods Hole Oceanographic Institute buildings used today were initially constructed in that era. The two enterprises were connected in mission yet separate in space. Whaling was centralized where WHOI is today, while the Guano Factory was set on the far side of Great Harbor.

For decades, the company thrived and even showcased its wares at the Philadelphia Centennial Exhibition of 1876. They were personally urged to display their wares by the secretary of the Smithsonian Institute.

Their posh and opulent Asian-Inspired pavilion became a rousing success at the first official World's Fair.

When the guano supply from the Howland Islands finally became depleted, the company acquired titles to the Chisholm's islands and some smaller islands off the coast of Honduras. Despite the benefits of greater community wealth and greater employment options, many folks in town without a strong financial connection disliked both the stench of the factory fumes and the concept behind the business model. Eventually, the company disbanded its production in 1889.

The Pacific Guano Company at Woods Hole. (Courtesy of Woods Hole Library.)

CAPTAIN ROWLAND CROCKER (1758–1852)
The Captain Who Stayed with His Ship

Roland's earlier life included a relatively long sojourn to France. As a holder of a "Letter of Marque" from the newly formed American Government in 1798, he was permitted the honor of seizing a foreign ship for the glory of his native land. Although officially undeclared, a state of war existed at sea between France and the United States. The profession of being a privateer was often seen as a very thin distinction between serving as a patriotic sailor for one's country or being a ruthless pirate in search of personal wealth.

Once in combat with a French ship, a musket ball pierced through his body, knocking him into a state of unconsciousness. His first mate surrendered the ship, which was then towed to France. In theory, upon recovery, he was a prisoner, but due to the political pressures of the day, he could roam the country at will with official permission. Indeed, he made the most of his French visit, which included a private audience with Napoleon Bonaparte. Their handshake was deemed more amicable than inhospitable while engaged in diplomatic talks.

When the trouble between the two countries settled, Crocker entered the merchant trade routes in 1807. In command of the ship *Otis*, he demonstrated great skill by navigating her half-wrecked sails through a gale into Dover Harbor. The *Otis* had been lying in anchor near the Downs in England. The Downs are part of the English Channel, near the Kent coast. Due to the force of a gale, she intertwined with a smaller frigate moored nearby. The crew was so nervous that they abandoned ship in a longboat, but Captain Crocker, with only a few loyal sailors, remained managing to stay aboard to sail the ship to safety. For his heroism, the vessel's underwriters rewarded him with a small tribute of a plaque and a sum of five hundred pounds. He was well prepared for the next step of his nautical career.

Roland Crocker was among the earliest packet captains sailing from 1820 to 1832, hailing from Falmouth. While serving as a seafarer, he authored *A Statement of Cases of Distress*. In this literary work, he refers to the kindness of providences permitting him to save the lives of thirty-two human beings from a watery grave. He earned a reputation for respecting humanity and would agree to deviate from his scheduled route to rescue a ship or assist a person in distress. Given the harsh business environment connected with packet schedules, the ship owners were certainly conflicted as their main allegiance to the strict rules of saving cargo seemed to take precedence over any personal concern for humanity.

He had crossed the ocean waves many more times than his peers, with over one hundred different trips noted. After he retired from shipping, his business acumen brought him into the insurance business. He moved his residence to New Bedford. He became so well known in the local area that he was elected to the House of Representatives. He combined insurance with his political life until he died in 1852.

MARY CHIPMAN LAWRENCE (1818–1892)
A Wife's Perspective on Whaling

In a beautifully written journal with wonderful prose and deep reflection, a journey of four and one-half years aboard the *Addison* comes vividly into view. She starts the first trip with apprehension and dread, fearing for the safety of herself, her five-year-old daughter, and her husband, Samuel. She returns a wiser person with a deeper respect for the sea at the very end. "I shall feel badly, after all, to give up my *Addison h*ome. It would be folly to think of spending four years less happily than the ones I have spent here."

Along the way, she honed her fishing skills. When she landed some of the larger species such as porpoise, tuna, or flying fish, the crew occasionally assisted her. Her notes on the beauty and splendor of the ocean reflect her admiration for sea life. She records a few months later: "I flatter myself that I have become quite a sailor." She had now spent so much time at sea she was less than confident that she would know how to reacquaint herself into the social graces of her gender once she returned to shore.

Taking a wife into the upper Pacific Artic Seas demanded fortitude. Mary was a rare exception as many captains refused to bring their wives to this arduous climate. The rain, fog, and chill permeated the air. Mary was content with the tasks assigned to her. In one instance, she did witness the drowning of an eighteen-year-old Portuguese crewman, which shook her to the core. She had taken such a liking to the boy that she pursued adoption.

The death that shook her the most was a more personal one. When the ship was put ashore on one voyage, she read that her father had passed. This news hit her dramatically as she felt so distant from her parents living in Sandwich. She grieved for a major portion of the remaining voyage. She enjoyed entertaining, and when the situation would present itself, she would invite other seafaring families to a festive meal. She also noted with an eerie foreboding that the whaling industry would have a short life. At one point, she observed that there were so many whalers present in this one confined area that the whales could never settle down, creating too much chaos. Overfishing combined with an undersupply of whales seemed to catch up with its eventual demise.

Her sea legs grew stronger. Near the end of one trip, she says: "Here is where I belong." The final tally for this excursion produced 2,500 barrels of oil and thousands of pounds of whalebone. A total of $50,000 was raised in the entire sale, which delighted the owners. Her husband's share of $3,600 was a handsome sum for those days.

This voyage would become Captain Lawrence's last whaling adventure. During the Civil War, he agreed to deliver food supplies as needed to Union troops. His ability to run a blockade was evident. Mary never regretted her participation in ocean travel, believing that the education afforded to her daughter, Minnie was extremely valuable. All the Lawrence family members are buried in Oak Grove Cemetery in Falmouth.

CAPTAIN SILAS JONES (1814–1896)
The Dangers of Whaling

Often there was palpable danger in Whaling. The whales and storms frequently broke up whaleboats. In many cases, men drowned or became entangled in their lines. Captain John Tobey of East Falmouth, who captained many a whaling vessel including *VIICOS* and *Awashmonks,* had to amputate his toes after a cask fell directly on him with gangrene settling in. Hostile natives attacked *Awashollks* on her second Pacific voyage. The captain was attempting to trade with the natives on the atoll of Nemarik, where the ship was attacked and overwhelmed. Many of the crew, the captain, and the first and second mate were all killed.

The nineteen-year-old Silas Jones was the third mate. At that time, he took command, bringing the ship safely back to Honolulu. Upon entering the port, he quickly turned back the ship's command to the United States Consulate in Hawaii. His personal belief was that it was inappropriate and improper to take command of a ship based on his young age and lack of experience. He was not sure that he held the full confidence of the crew. Nonetheless, his ship logs told the story of bravery and skill in difficult waters.

Despite his reservations, his reputation indeed grew solidly. Only four years later, at the age of twenty-three, he took official command of the *Hobomok a*nd later the *Commodore Morris.* After sailing on the *Commodore Morris,* the boat was sold to a New Bedford fishing fleet. This exchange would mark it as the final active whaling boat to sail out

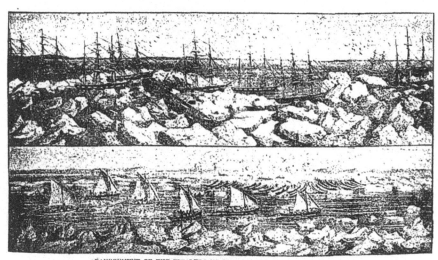

ABANDONMENT OF THE WHALERS IN THE ARCTIC IN 1871, FROM OLD PRINT.
Upper Picture Shows Vessels Caught in Ice. Lower Picture Sho wa Camp of Crews the First Night After Leaving Their Vessels.

Frozen Artic Whaling Fleet in 1871, Boston Globe, *April 11, 1915.*

of Falmouth Harbor. Later his whaling ship, the *Awashollks*, became part of the frozen fleet lost in the frozen Artic Sea. The *Awashmonk* was caught in the 1871 Artic Sea Freeze. In all, thirty-three whaling vessels froze that winter and were left abandoned. This incident dealt a heavy blow to the whaling industry, experiencing a sharp decline.

CAPTAIN SOLOMON L. HAMLIN (1827–1898)
Sailor and Proprietor of Falmouth-by-the-Sea

Solomon L. Hamlin was born in Teaticket in April of 1827. He was the son of Simeon and Nancy (Lawrence) and a grandson of Deacon. Solomon Lawrence. He proudly carried the name "Lawrence" as his middle name as a sign of respect for his heritage.

Solomon was a shipmaster for thirty years, from 1840 until 1870. His voyages were mostly whaling, with an occasional commercial venture added as time allowed. One of his favorite ships was the bark *Eugenia* which came out of New Bedford. Unlike some of his peers, he frequented New Zealand and Australian waters. There may have been fewer whales noted in this region, but there was an even bigger reward when the competition for whalers was kept to a reasonable number.

The port records of Falmouth harbor indicate that he took out the whaler *Catalpa*, heading for the Galapagos Islands. His return with whale oil was one of the largest catches ever recorded as he traveled and saw items of a most peculiar and attractive nature. He started to harbor the idea of bringing novelty items back to Cape Cod. He wondered if there would be a market for both domestic needs with a small touch of demand for exotic things with an international flair.

Upon his retirement from the sea, he decided to open a shop called Falmouth-by-the-Sea, with an unofficial title of "The Naples of America". During his various nautical jaunts, he came to appreciate the process of international trading. He learned that the ancient marketplace of Naples was an epicenter for renaissance wares. His store carried both American-made products such as Ivory soap and British teas and Pacific Island

Falmouth-by-the-Sea, shop of Captain Hamlin. (Courtesy of the Falmouth Historic Society.)

jams. It is difficult to ascertain if his store was ever very profitable. His kindly nature and generous nature would prompt him to be overly generous to his loyal customers. If he knew of any familial hardships, he would consider offering discount prices or even potential loan forgiveness.

His oldest son, William, followed in his footsteps as a sea captain, but he unfortunately never returned from a Pacific whaling expedition. Two other sons, Simeon and Edward B., were given the maintenance of the store. His funeral in 1898 reflected the funeral customs of the day. The ceremony was held at the family residence attended by an open door to all appreciative citizens. Reverend C.H. Washburn provided the eulogy, identifying him as a man of "most genial, social and hospitable spirit." A male quartet sang songs of wake, and the floral bouquet contributed by the community was both colorful and bright.

Harwich

Origin of the Town's Name

Its name comes from a seaside port near Essex, England. This specific British port was a familiar sight for newcomers from England, venturing towards the New England region. Rumor has it that a resident to the state assembly named Patrick Butler was considering this name while walking to Boston from Cape Cod to perform his appointed congressional duties. The General Court agreed to his suggestion. The southeastern part of Harwich became part of Orleans in 1772, and Brewster claimed some of the northwestern portion in 1802.

A Brief History

In 1694 when William and Mary were the monarchs of England, the Province of the Massachusetts Bay was established. The first governor was William Phips, who signed an act on Sept 14, 1694, declaring Harwich, Massachusetts, an incorporated town. Phips, himself, was born and raised in Maine. As a young seaman, he discovered one of the largest sunken treasure finds of gold and silver ever discovered. His appointment as governor came because of his leading pre-colonial America through the King William's War which pitted the emerging colony against the French and the Indians. The town came into being just two years after Governor Phips ended the Salem witchcraft trials based upon the advice of Increase Mather.

Notable Connection to the Sea

Every indicator shouts out a rich maritime heritage for the town of Harwich. The official United States Census for 1850 shows that 71% of Harwich males, age fifteen and older, were "mariners," or "master mariners," indicating that their work was directly aboard a ship or somehow connected to the sea.

Shipping vessels continued to grace Harwich harbors well into the nineteenth century. The book, *Harwich Vessels*, describes six hundred and twenty different ships having a Harwich connection from 1872 to 1900. The logbook is readily available with details and sketches on the world wide web. This research reflects only one major source, the *Harwich Independent News*. The research was sponsored by the Harwich Historical Society and is by no means an exhaustive effort in identifying ships.

CAPTAIN CALEB ALLEN (1834–1906)
The Corn Cracker

Coming from a long line of Harwich captains, Caleb was the son of Captain James Allen, who was a cannon expert during the Revolutionary War. As a typical youth of his day, he agreed to serve as a cabin boy on a fishing vessel, then later moved onto the role of second mate by the age of nineteen.

He was primarily a coastal captain who commanded the ship the *John F. Forman*. After five years as a shipmaster, he concluded that sponsoring ships willing to venture from Harwich to deep sea trading ports could make a greater profit. He decided to sell the *John F Forman* and turned to the ship brokerage business. His ancestor, Captain John Allen, in the 1750s, acquired seaside land, which he developed. This stretch of land was originally a shallow pond with a small space as an outlet to the ocean. Over the years, the shore was dredged many times, allowing larger ships to maneuver. Today, this site occupies the locale of the Allen Harbor Yacht Club and Marine Services.

His specific method of commercial shipping ventures would include an aspect of what we call today the "farm-to-table food chain." Despite a colloquial use of the term corn cracker to denote a person of lower economic means, sometimes of Southern heritage, in New England maritime use, he was proud to call himself a "Corn Cracker." During his era, this term was seen as a positive one, designating the acquisition of specific features of fresh produce to shipped in rapid time to various ports through maritime trading.

These sea captains typically owned their vessels. They frequently were either still active farmers, presently owning a farm, or having a strong connection to a range of local farmers. The captains would first go to nearby local harbors such as New Bedford or Providence, bringing local fresh farm products to the wharves. They returned to Harwich's ports with backyard goods, hardware, and various sorts of consigned merchandise.

JOB CHASE (1776–1863)
A Sailor with a Strong Business Acumen

As a leader of the maritime industry, a new dynasty of captains emerged. In his first marriage, he was proud of his nine children. Of these, six sons were lost at sea. Four of the six were masters of their own vessels. In the later years of the 1790s, he commanded a fleet of vessels that his sons and close relatives would use for deep-sea shipping. He and his sons would engage in various trade endeavors such as taking mahogany from Santo Domingo to Boston for home construction, or bringing passengers going from Darien, Connecticut, to the Caribbean or even retrieving sheep's skin from Nantucket for general consumption.

Many of his ships were connected to the name of Hope with titles such as *Hope's Lady*, *Hope and Phoebe*, *New Hope*, *Old Hope*, and even the *Hope for Peace*. He was known far and wide as being a successful merchant. Due to his acquired wealth, Boston politicians would plead with him to financially support various candidates such as Samuel Lothrop for Governor.

Although he did engage in some European trade, the bulk of his fortune was made with shorter maritime trips that brought more profitable based on greater volume. For him, the reward was much more about the value of shorter trips with targeted results than the larger profit of year-long ocean excursions. One of his notable skills was having the ability to be flexible in his overall trading perspective. For instance, one of his captains originally planned to bring barrels from Baltimore to Boston. He concluded that going from North Carolina to Barbados directly for lumber would be a much more expedient means to collect that supply and engage in other trading types of trade commodities.

In 1842, he built his wharf and built the eighty-five-ton schooner *Job Chase* from timber cut upon his lands. Other vessels were built at Hamden, Maine, and Dartmouth. During the length of his commercial trading business, he managed to fit out a large fleet. His sons, Job and Sears, were responsible for maintaining his business.

He was particularly interested in public affairs and the affairs of the church. He served his town as a selectman and was a representative from Harwich to the state legislature. With materials, finances, and practical support, he became one of the original stockholders and founders of the old Yarmouth Bank. In its day, this bank was one of the busiest of local enterprises, giving employment to many men, building up the capital of West Harwich.

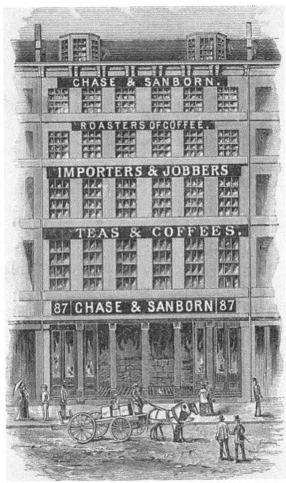

Chase and Sanborn Company, 87 Broad Street, Boston, Massachusetts. (Courtesy of Chase & Sanborn.)

His son, Caleb Chase, was responsible for making coffee a worldwide phenomenon. Chase & Sanborn Coffee is an American coffee brand created by the same coffee roasting importing company, established in 1862 in Boson, Massachusetts, with the assistance of James Solomon Sanborn (1835–1903). It claims to be the first coffee company to pack and ship roasted coffee in sealed tins worldwide.

The start of the end of the Job Chase's fleet began in 1836 when his son Jonathon wrote, "I think it's time to quit owning ships as we now own. There appears to be jealousy within the management." The Chase fleet greatly diminished that same year, and a lively family business left Harwich.

VALENTINE DOANE (1804–1892)
From Sailor to Bank President

Coming from Harwichport, Doane was always surrounded by the sea. He worked as a cleaner and cook aboard fishing expeditions at a very young age. For over twenty years, he captained several vessels. In 1845, his mission turned to the fishing enterprise, becoming an owner and outfitter of many local vessels. In 1865, his fishing empire was reported to be at its height. He was looked upon as a national leader within his profession.

He opened a general grocery store near his residence, which became a popular spot to purchase flour, corn, and grain. His deep respect for the fishing empire and generosity beamed brightly as he sponsored many related literary efforts. As president of the Seaman's Friend Society of Harwich, his organization donated books and bibles to over one hundred seamen serving aboard sixteen different vessels.

He was also a deeply religious figure who believed that the Sabbath day on a ship should be excluded from work as a time for prayer and reflection. His fishing fleet would conduct bible readings and hold weekly religious services, which all crew members were expected to attend.

In *Cape Cod Magazine*, there was a report on how whales were endangered because of carelessly flung anchors. One of his ships in 1855 accidentally struck a whale. The mammal struggled to free itself, eventually succeeding. Nonetheless, the whale died a few hours later from extreme fatigue. In a *Bulletin of the Bureau of Fishing*, he recounts a voyage along the Newfoundland shoreland. He commented favorably on the demeanor, industry, and kindness of these Canadian people. The village men would fish with dispatch and diligence while the woman would clean and cure the product at home.

He would often comment on the various local culinary tastes relative to fishermen. He once noticed that Cape Cod men would love to feast on oysters and clams while the Newfoundland men who accidentally harvested them in their net would merely discard them as waste. He left a considerable fortune and his entire fishing industry as an inheritance to his son, Valentine Doane, Junior, who kept the business thriving into the start of the twentieth century.

Upon retirement from the sea in 1844, he diversified into several types of business. He and others organized an initiative to build Marshbank Wharf in 1847, which the fishing industry appreciated and rapidly increased due to the construction of this facility.

He also took an active part in the erection of the Pilgrim Church. As a religious figure, he was known for his sympathy and pecuniary aid to the unfortunate. His astute financial sense was omnipresent. He would become the director of the Yarmouth National Bank, the Barnstable County Insurance Co., and the Dennis and Harwich Marine Insurance Company.

CAPTAIN JONATHAN WALKER (1799–1878)
"The Man with the Branded Hand"

Jonathan was raised a farmer's son in Harwich, Massachusetts. Farming in this part of Cape Cod was particularly difficult due to its dry soil composition. Unlike many other sea captains, Jonathan was the first in his family to set sail around the globe. He would be the first male Walker from a family of ten males to sail. At the age of seventeen, he left home.

He once sailed seven runaway slaves around the peninsula of Florida in the summer of 1844. The slaves wished to reach the Bahamas to seek the freedom of another nation for these African American men. They almost reached their goal but were captured just a half-day journey from their selected port. The slaves were returned to their masters, but not before escaping the whipping of the jailer who imprisoned Walker and the slaves, leaving them on a dirty cell floor. One of the slaves died on this spot.

He spent a full year in jail and participated in two different trials in the US court system as a slave sympathizer. He was first severely fined financially, locked into a pillory, and eventually branded by a US Marshall with a hot iron ordered by the court. The two letters 'SS" (slave stealer) were permanently attached to his right wrist showing the world that this man was not to be trusted and irrevocably labeled as an enemy of the state. His punishment was the only one of this type of sentence ever administered in the annals of court trials.

He was an ardent abolitionist sixty years before the Civil War. His story continues after this bodily disfigurement in 1846. He would eventually move to Michigan and Wisconsin, on the edge of Northwest expansion. Overall, migration was moving west during this period. He became a noted and respected speaker against the cause of slavery. His wisdom and personal courage were cited as a vital rationale fueling the fires of a national reckoning to end this tyrannical treatment of mankind. His deeds became the subject of a poem by John Greenleaf Whittier as his exploits were cited and extolled. "He became the man with a branded hand."

In the mid-1840s, Jonathan Walker began a new career as a spokesperson for the abolitionist movement. Along with Frederick Douglas, he toured the nation condemning the evil perpetrated onto a whole race of people. He spoke in town halls from Plymouth to Mattapoisett, explaining his rationale for his actions and the punitive treatment he had received from contrary ideological forces. He authored a book titled *Chattelized Humanity, Horses, Slaves, and Other Cattle*. He realized a need to expand beyond the current Eastern Coast base, aiming to preach his anti-slavery message to the new territories forming in the country. This action would lead to his relocation to Wisconsin.

As he once watched a slave trade in operation in the Midwest, he was quoting as saying, "My heart aches to see the slave children being torn away from their family." The concept of separate bidders for one united family was one specific evil within a complex of other treacherous behaviors he could not abide by.

A second book he authored was called *A Picture of Slavery for Youth*. He concluded that the best way to reach the mind of new citizens about the evils of slavery was when minds were young and still in their formative years. He worked diligently to have every schoolhouse pick up this somber message in reading this novel.

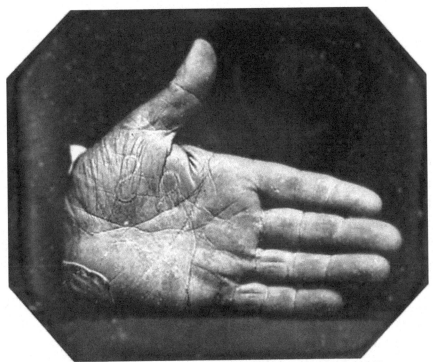

An 1845 daguerreotype of Walker's branded hand by photographers Southworth and Hayes.

Mashpee

Origin of the Town's Name

The town›s name anglicizes an Algonquian name, "mass-nippe." Mass is «great» or "greater," and nippe is «water," such as Massachusetts meaning at the "greatest hill."

A Brief History

This ancient Indian territory is an incorporated commonwealth district containing almost sixteen square miles. This tract was procured for the indigenous people by Mr. Richard Bourne, a native of England. After he arrived at Sandwich, he began to focus his labors on the temporal and spiritual good of the indigenous people. After having obtained the above deed, Bourne pursued his evangelical work, and he was ordained pastor in 1670. He was called to minister to the local indigenous people, charged with converting them to Christianity.

The colonists designated Mashpee on Cape Cod as the largest native reservation in Massachusetts. The name can also be translated as "the greater cove" or "great pond," where the term water is referenced as greater at one end than another.

The British Crown designated Mashpee as a planation against the will of the Wampanoag people. The colony gave the indigenous people the so-called "right" to elect their own officials to maintain their area but otherwise subjected them to the regulations of the colonial government. The population of the plantation declined steadily due to the strict conditions placed upon the Wampanoag people, avoiding the obligation to tend to their medical or physical needs.

In 1777, permission was obtained from England to sell small parcels of lands outside of the jurisdiction of the Native Territory. Mashpee, originally spelled Marshpee, lies south of Sandwich and is bounded on the south by the ocean.

Notable Connection to the Sea

Being closely associated with the Wampanoag tribe, the confines of Mashpee lie within two large bays—Waquoit Bay between Falmouth and Mashpee and Popponesset between Mashpee and Barnstable. These spots were ideal locations for the viability of fishing and whaling options in the region.

In pre-colonial days, natives would occasionally fish using their dugout boats and later, under English dominance, were, in essence, duped into serving as whalers. Natives represented an available, inexpensive labor force. In essence, Cape Cod maritime history starts here. The young Wampanoag men were sent to whale in large numbers. The Wampanoags of Aquinnah held an annual religious whaling ceremony known as "the Powdawe." The chief would venture out to first block off the whale's forward progress, followed by a series of smaller boats to surround the creature. Then, the whale would be driven directly to shore as the natives prayed and rejoiced.

By the 1760s, it is estimated that two-thirds of the younger males from the Wampanoag tribe, men in their thirties or younger, were creatively coerced into a life at sea. Bookkeeping became a vehicle to indenture young Native men. All residents, both colonists and indigenous people, shopped for their basic goods from local merchants who kept careful written records of goods received and money owed. Using cryptic scrawls and customized shorthand notes, account books held the record for what every family must pay. Using words such as "Sundry" and "Gigkot," families were assigned various levels of financial liabilities.

Before the American Revolution, indigenous men and slaves comprised most of the crews on whaling ships. Repayment of debts became a novel way for whaling crews to be formed. Once an amount reached a certain level, the parents of the native men were directed to make good on their line of credit. The local people could satisfy their payment for the full family debt owed by agreeing to a contract stating their son would agree to serve as a crew member. Once aboard a ship, there were several ways that the contracts could be renewed or even kept as a perpetual payment plan that needed further attention.

At first, most native men willingly agreed to their conscription, believing that they were heroes saving their family from ruin. In other cases, a signing bonus was introduced. After the initial agreement was reached, some natives frequently grew weary of their commitment. Sensing their hesitation, natives were permitted to ask for additional incentives. Ship owners granted occasional personal requests, even silly ones, such as "seven more hats" or "five pounds of soap." If all else failed, an inducement of strong spirits could also weaken their resolve. Beyond questionable recruitment techniques, their promised share of the earned profits at the end of the voyage was either minimalized or perhaps never even given for a host of sketchy reasons, such as the ship's failure to reach overall profit goals.

BENJAMIN BRADLEY (1836–1902)
First Black Boat Designer of Note

Benjamin Bradley was born into slavery in Anne Arundel, Maryland, in March 1836. It has been theorized that he acquired his literacy while learning from his master's children. According to the Maryland State Manumission records, Bradley's owner was John T. Hammond.

As a teenager, Bradley worked at a printing office. He showed ingenuity and mechanical skills by the age of sixteen. He built a steam engine out of a gun barrel, pewter, round steel, and various materials. His master was so impressed, he got him a job as a helper in the Department of Natural and Experimental Philosophy at the Naval Academy at Annapolis. At Annapolis, Bradley worked as a general helper. According to the *African Repository* of 1859, he was paid in full for his work, but the money he had made went directly to his master, who allowed Bradley to keep five dollars a month for himself. As a helper at the academy, Bradley helped establish science experiments involving chemical gases.

It is mentioned that his professors at the Naval Academy were very fascinated with him. Professor Hopkins of the Naval Academy wrote about Bradley's work as a helper at the Academy. He wrote that he would set up experiments rapidly. He was a quick learner, declaring that "he always looks for the scientific law by which things act." Professor

Hopkins's children taught Bradley how to read and write and do math such as algebra and geometry.

Bradley built a steam engine and sold it to the midshipmen during his time at the Naval Academy. With the money he earned from selling the steam engine and the money saved while working at the Naval Academy, he designed a steam engine large enough to run the first mechanical sloop of war that could exceed 16 knots an hour. He sold this model engine to a classmate from the Naval Academy and then used the proceeds to build the "first steam-powered warship." Because he was enslaved, Bradley was never allowed to receive a patent for the engine he developed. He was, however, able to sell it. He used the profits, plus the money given to him by professors at the Naval Academy, to obtain his freedom at the cost of $1000. According to Maryland state records, Bradley was manumitted from his owner, John T. Hammond, on September 30, 1859, in the County of Anne Arundel, Maryland.

The U.S. Naval Academy was relocated to Newport, Rhode Island, during the Civil War. According to the *African Repository* for August 1865, Bradley was employed as a freeman at the U.S. Naval Academy in

Wood engraving of US Naval Academy in 1853. (Courtesy US Naval Records, attributed to William Rickerby Miller.)

Rhode Island, where he worked under the supervision of Professor A.W. Smith. There Bradley continued his work on constructing small steam engines and continued to show his ingenuous mechanical skills. He worked as an instructor in the Philosophical Department at the Naval Academy in 1864. He was given credit for designing and constructing a "miniature steam engine and boiler about 6-fly power."

According to the 1900 US Census, Bradley was sixty-four years old and living in Mashpee, Massachusetts. His occupation was described as a "philosophical lecturer." The census also indicated that he was married to Gertrude Bradley living with her for nineteen years, with whom he had three children.

Seventeen-Year-Old Whaler, AARON KEELER (1803–1856)
An Indigenous Whaler

It was not unusual for parents or court-appointed guardians to secure the services of Mashpee natives to work as sailors, particularly whalers. In 1820, many natives were assigned to ships as indentured slaves. These young men would work long hours and perform dangerous tasks while serving at sea, often for long periods.

One of the most devious devices used by local entrepreneurs would be extending a line of credit to native people, then permitting them to pay off their debt either through hard labor or a written contract. Thus, Aaron Keeler, with the consent of his mother and the recognized state guardian of the Mashpee Indians, worked aboard the whaler, *Dauphin*, sailing out of Nantucket. Shares of the final profits would be sold on a pre-arranged basis. Captain Freeman Percival embarked upon a three-year voyage to the Pacific Ocean for a one-hundred-dollar fee and the removal of all debts incurred by his mother.

The written agreement reads as follows:

> March 18, 1820
> This document certified that I approve of the contract of Freeman Percival and my son Aaron to perform a whale voyage to Cape Horn for the consideration certified in the written obligation for him.

This document was signed both by Lydia (Pocknett) Keeler and N. Marston, Overseer of Mashpee.

Aaron also signed a document that he, as a minor, was in full agreement with the contract, and if for any reason, he failed to appear as promised, a new debt of $500 would be assigned to the mother, and the burden of my family. Once a commitment was made, Direct coercion of native people was not necessarily the only inducement for sailing on Native whaling ships, but research indicates that it did occur. In reviewing the crew of Mashpee residents, Native men and some enslaved African Americans were overrepresented in the overall population.

Once aboard, Aaron had a most striking experience; his ship came across a stranded starving sailor of the *Essex*. This was the same ship rammed by a whale, forcing all the sailors to seek refuge on a small remote island in the pacific near Chile without vegetation or animals. The rescued crew was brought aboard the *Dauphine* while Aaron and other crew members nursed the stranded men back to some degree of health and safety. He learned that an extremely bizarre case of cannibalism to remain alive befell the survivors of the *Essex*.

A sad reality was that often the natives were typically underpaid or only paid a small percentage of what they were entitled to receive. Sometimes the investors claimed that a sufficient profit was not realized, or perhaps some other type of extenuating circumstance existed within the contract. Even worse than the meager pay issue, natives were the first people called to do the most dangerous tasks on the ship, such as climbing high above the sails in windy conditions or diving deep within the ocean to perform duties. Their mortality rate at sea was much higher than their European counterparts.

WILLIAM APEES (1798–1839)
The Mashpee Revolt of 1833, Protector of Indigenous Whalers
Born in 1798 in western Massachusetts of the Pequod tribe, he experienced a miserable childhood. Raised by an abusive grandmother, he became a ward of the state at age six. He later worked as an indentured servant for the Furman family of Connecticut. With this family, he was

well educated and attended school for six years, where he concurrently would learn the trade of cooperage.

He later joined the United States Army at the age of fifteen and observed that the government rarely treated all soldiers with a similar degree of respect. For example, all active-duty personnel were promised a bonus salary under certain conditions. However, white soldiers were uniformly rewarded while his native peers only occasionally received an equal amount. Based on their open acceptance, he was drawn to the Methodist faith. Since the church invited all races to participate, he felt most comfortable learning more about their religious tenets. Acquiring public speaking skills, he was much in demand as a public speaker preaching the good news and principles of Methodism.

In 1829, he published an autobiography titled, *A Son of the Forest*. Within this book, he detailed the outrageous ways Wampanoag women were mistreated and how his native people were often exposed to and encouraged to partake of "strong spirits." Then under the influence of alcohol, their rights and properties were often seized. In that same year of 1829, the state overseers of Mashpee were conspiring with local Cape Cod sea captains to secure the services of all the young Wampanoag men to serve on merchant boats and whaling expeditions. He heard these rumors of injustice and decided himself to verify their veracity. This was a perfect confrontation. On the one hand, you have a well-educated, articulate native with literary and strong speaking skills matched against unscrupulous court-appointed overseers determined to pad their pockets.

He arrived on the scene and offered his services to the Mashpee tribe. He requested that the tribe accept him into their fold which they were most willing to do. One of the first injustices that he noticed was that Harvard was sending down a local clergyman who worked diligently with European descendants but overlooked the inclusion of Native inhabitants.

At first, the local newspapers were most receptive to publishing his remarks. Sympathy was indeed building for the poor treatment shown to the Mashpee tribe. His speeches were fully documented and well represented. Based on his efforts, several resolutions were created and presented to the overseers and local courts:

- Resolved that we will rule ourselves in line with the constitution that declares that all men are born free and equal in status

- Resolved we will not permit any white man to come into our plantation to cut wood and hay for their use without prior agreement or take any Native sons to work for debts incurred

- Resolved that the native people will be able to worship as they please and allowed to attend Harvard-sponsored ministry if they so choose.

Then in 1836, Minister Apees was asked to eulogize the historic efforts of King Philip, commemorating his century-old indigenous uprising. His review was circulated throughout the country. His comparison of the Chief to General George Washington was particularly offensive. Harvard University never allowed the indigenous people to attend his religious services, nor was there ever much respect given to any existing laws respecting native peoples' rights. In the end, his heavy drinking plagued him, often making him appear foolish. His followers lost their

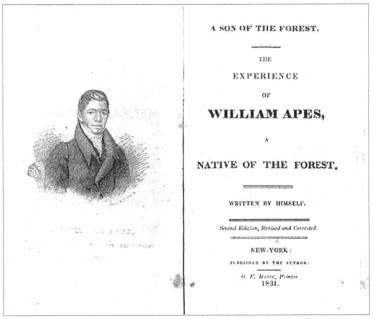

Book by William Apee, The Experience of William Apes: A Native of the Forest.

collective energy to defend him. He died a poor man in New York City a short time later.

The Composite Duties of the Wampanoag Whaler from Mashpee

Rather than discussing just one specific whaler from Mashpee, we can glean a composite view in analyzing the research of others. A visiting French traveling scholar, Hector St. John de Crevecoeur, visited Mashpee in the 1760s. He recorded several direct interviews with Wampanoag families. Piecing together his written notes makes it possible to gain a clearer picture of how whaling was organized in the 1700s and even in the 1600s. We see three concrete operations that, when bound together, provide a better understanding of the whole whaling process:

- At first, a crew needs to be secured. His notes reflect that the natives were every bit as capable as the European descendants in terms of their overall skills, abilities, and courage. Three out of every five men would be of native heritage in a typical ship. The vessels most appropriate would be a brig of about 150 tons in size, particularly used for longer ocean hunts. A minimum of two smaller boats would be on board with a crew of six men. Four men would man the oars while one standing on the bow as the harpooner and a second man at the helm supplied verbal instructions.

- Two boats were necessary if the first attack boat was overturned, and the men needed rescue. Most of these initial boats carried Native men. The crew has no direct wages. Each man draws a share as per their written sailing contract. These men never exceeded the age of forty as strength, agility, and unquestionable loyalty must be present.

- As soon as the ship enters an area where whales might be sighted, a man is sent up to sit near the tip of the mast head. If one is seen, he cries out, "Awaite Pawana (Here is a whale)." In less than six minutes, two boats are lowered with all equipment at the ready. They begin rowing towards the whale. Natives typically performed this dangerous part of the hunt.

Oil painting of the dangers of whaling, artist unknown. (Courtesty of New England Historical Society.)

SOLOMON ATTAQUIN (1810–1895)
A Wampanoag Hotel Owner

Solomon Jr. was born to Solomon senior. The elder was a strong advocate for the rights of the Wampanoags. There are records on three separate occasions that legal petitions were filed with the Massachusetts courts between the years 1780 and 1795 in which infringements of rights were cited on their ability to self-govern as independent people.

Solomon kept the tradition alive of protecting indigenous people. He first started as a young cook on long whaling excursions. His cooking became so popular and well-known with the crew that he was often recruited to repeat these duties many times over.

When he eventually retired from whaling jaunts, his reputation for great food preparation led him to a new career. The Attaquin Hotel in Mashpee was born in 1840. The hotel was located where the community gardens are now on Route 130/Main Street, across from Lake Avenue.

In the 1840s, the hotel was more than a place to rest. It was considered a social club, watering hole, clubhouse, and spot to relax to meet relatives, friends, celebrities, hunters, fishermen, historians, and even

anthropologists. It was known that many writers studying the treatment
of the indigenous people formed the basis of their writing and continued
their education of the Wampanoag at the Attaquin Hotel.

Research at the Mashpee Archives says the hotel had two bars, one
for the natives and one for non-natives. Once customers settled in for a
few libations, they would mingle while drinking. The preferred beverages
of the day were Pickwick Ale, a spirit known as "sea diver whiskey' and
perhaps a final shot of Four Roses. In those days, Mashpee was over
ninety-nine percent Mashpee Wampanoag living there. Celebrated visitors came, such as Joseph Jefferson, President Grover Cleveland, Daniel
Webster, and Henry David Thoreau.

From a traditional perspective, many traditional Cape Cod clambakes were held on the grounds behind the Attaquin. People would come
from all over Cape Cod to enjoy the clams, mussels, lobster, and all of the
clambakes' healthiest foods. Solomon Attaquin sold the hotel in 1888
and spent his remaining few years living at the site.

The census report in 1892 for Solomon Attatquin listed his position
in three ways. He served as a general mariner, the town's postmaster, and
the Mashpee selectman. He was admired for his constant devotion to
attending to the Wampanoag people's needs in his life as a politician and
a hotel owner.

Orleans

Origin of the Town's Name

Why do you suppose a small town on Cape Cod might choose the same name as a city on the Loire River in France? The best evidence points to Captain Isaac Snow. In 1780, while the colonists were still at war with England, Isaac Snow served aboard the ship *Resolution*. British forces seized his vessel, and he was taken to a prison in Plymouth, England. Wishing to return to the American fight, he escaped spending considerable time in Europe, mostly by walking. He eventually managed to find a way to book passage to a slightly more friendly environment in France.

There, he met Compte d'Estaing and the Marquis de Lafayette, two very popular figures during the American Revolution. Both Frenchmen strongly defended the rise of democratic governments to rise in the world. Upon his return to the Cape, he suggested this specific section of Eastham be named Orleans to honor the bold spirit of Frenchmen who fought for independence. It is also worth noting that the ideology of Lafayette, a member of European nobility, who denounced a privileged life to fight for a new country, was also held in high esteem by the American people cementing our common bond with the French people.

A Brief History

The earliest inhabitants were the Nausets, a tribe of the Wampanoag people. They were, by all accounts, friendly and agreeable people who lived in peace and harmony along the sea. However, in 1614, six years before the Pilgrim landing, other travelers from Europe graced their shores. Encountering a new strain of virus brought by newcomers proved deadly for the indigenous people. Records indicate that between the interval of 1614 and 1619, almost two-thirds of the indigenous people died of disease. Beginning with the start of colonialization, a strong reason for distrust, intentional or not, arose between the existing tribes and new European arrivals.

In one situation, when one child of the Puritans strayed too far from home, a panic ensued. The goodwill of a Nauset search party rescued the young lad, returning him safely to his parents. From that point on, the two groups slightly eased their tensions, slowly learning about each other ways. There were persuasive attempts to Christianize the local people. Great strides occurred in their proselytizing, with many Natives becoming aware of the word in the Christian gospel.

Within the original settlers, seven families became dismissive of the many restrictive Puritan ways; they wished to assert their independence, practicing slightly different tenets of the religion. Six of these families were Prence, Doane, Bangs, Smalley, Cook, and Higgins. These families left the Plymouth Colony and migrated to the Eastham shore. For 152 years, Eastham was the official name of this region.

The seventh family, of Nicholas Snow, was also part of this separatist group, but he settled his home more towards the present-day Orleans portion of Eastham. He would rightfully become a central figure in settlement of Orleans. He became the village's first tax collector, a local constable, and a central authority figure to whom citizens reported in this newly founded region

In March of 1797, governmental action changed the town's political structure. Orleans was already acting quite independently from Eastham in their way of doing business. On March 3rd, 1797, an act to divide the Southern Parish from Eastham into a town named Orleans was signed by Governor Samuel Adams. Soon after that, the first town meeting was established when Hezekiah Higgins and Heman Linnell were picked to serve as selectmen. Orleans had about one thousand citizens, while Eastham had around 475.

The Act of 1797 specified that a "principle inhabitant" should be selected as a governmental representative. Hezekiah Higgins became the choice of the people as selectman. Notes from one of the first town meeting records indicate that ten fish wardens were hired to insure clean water passages. Three districts in town were zoned for education, each having its own school building. Three hundred dollars were put aside for religious instruction, and three hundred and sixty dollars were approved to help the poor.

A Notable Connection to the Sea

The Battle of Rock Harbor occurred on December 19, 1814. Some might consider it a minor skirmish, but to the local people of Cape Cod, it was a satisfying victory against British forces. The War of 1812 threatened all the East Coast. Since Britain was also at war with France, supplies were scarce, and additional resources were desperately sought. British vessels traveled the New England coast seizing both privateers and commercial ships alike as prizes for their own needs.

From the American perspective, our new nation needed to act decisively to be seen as a sovereign nation. We were no longer colonists and should not be bound to British demands of any type. Cape Cod was particularly vulnerable to naval encounters due to its geographic contours and the shallow depth of the inlets. A shipping blockade around the cape shore could keep local ships in a treacherous spot. His Majesty's Ship, the *Newcastle,* was a fifty-gun fourth-rated vessel of the Royal Navy. Stationed near Wellfleet, its fire power was immense. This ship saw service during the Napoleonic Wars and on the American coast.

Wishing to secure control of the bayside of Cape Cod, the British sent out messengers to several coastal towns demanding a financial ransom lest the destruction of valuable harbors and saltworks would ensue. Eastham and Brewster both agreed to pay for this protection. The proud people of Orleans never succumbed to pay the one-thousand-pound request. While the *Newcastle* was temporarily partially grounded on a Wellfleet Bar, British soldiers under the command of Frederick Marriott ventured to Orleans with orders to toss products into the sea and burn up town-owned properties. The British removed masts and spars to lighten the ship's load, making it seaworthy once again. They placed the ship's material to the side, seeking to reclaim them later. Orleans residents found these hidden rafts promptly, burning them to the ground.

When the angered British forces came ashore in a longboat, they burnt three local sloops on the bayside as a retaliatory act. The residents of Brewster and Eastham joined in the fight, lining up on the shore with muskets ready. It was certain that at least one British sailor was shot and killed. Their resistance proved so strong that it hastened a rapid retreat to their main vessel. Although not a major military victory, it was certainly an emphatic moment of euphoria for the local town people and a bright symbol of American resilience. The naval blockade around the Cape was hindered, and their threatening actions were repelled.

ISAAC SNOW (1759–1856)
Captured Prisoner of the Revolutionary War, Ally of Lafayette

Isaac was born in 1759 on Brick Hill Road. His first few years, his life was spent in farming. In 1777, he enlisted in the Massachusetts Militia. At first, he served with Captain Isiah Higgins at Dorchester Heights and later with Colonel Josiah Whitney in South Kingston, Rhode Island.

Later, the lure of sea life attracted him. He agreed to serve as a crew member on the *Resolution,* a mid-sized American vessel of ten guns. This ship was assigned to patrol along the East coast to prevent British ships and privateers from causing havoc. Their specific mission backfired when they were seized nine days out of port.

The crew was taken to Old Mill Prison, a grim and forbidding structure in Plymouth, England. Isaac was very impressed with the humane treatment provided to the American prisoners. The food was adequate; their treatment was seen as benign. They even provide educational courses for all prisoners. He learned the skill of cobbling, which he would make great use of when he reached the later part of his life.

At one point, he was transferred to a prison ship off the coast of Portugal. This move proved to be very practical and beneficial to him. He and some other prisoners took advantage of their maritime knowledge and hid during the day in the confines of the vessel., They were able to swim to shore to reach dry land. These men were hardy. Hearing that the famous Marquis de Lafayette could be found in Orleans, they arrived there on foot. The Compte d'Estang met them, introducing them to the Marquis.

The British frigate *Somerset* was stationed at Provincetown harbor during the start of the American Revolutionary War. Britain demanded that every horse or cow that could be seized was deemed spoils of war to be claimed by troops. Farmers in Orleans knew that their livestock was in grave danger, so a process of evasive hiding animals ensued. In November 1778, a major storm caught the ship on Truro's outer bars. As a result of the wreck, one-third of the crew drowned, and 480 survivors were captured jointly by soldiers from Provincetown

When he returned home at the junction of Pochet and Barley Neck Road in East Orleans, he was received locally as a war hero. He became both the miller and a part-owner of the East Orleans Millwork. In addition to the milling, he also performed cobbling services for residents. He was able to outlive many of his fellow Revolutionary War veterans living to ninety-seven. Being a favorite son, he was instrumental in suggesting a new name for the region that was previously called Eastham.

MR. JOSHUA CROSBY (1741–1824)
Cannoneer for the USS *Constitution*, "Old Ironsides"

Joshua Crosby was thirteen when he first went to sea on a pink-stern schooner to fish Georges Bank, eighty miles southeast of Orleans. His ship ventured out from Nauset Harbor. Once he tasted sea life, he would spend the greater part of his life on the ocean, initially on long whaling voyages, then aboard coastal trading schooners. He served as a mate gunner during our nation's conflict with Tripoli.

In the summer of 1812, he enlisted to serve on *Old Ironsides*, the USS *Constitution*, under the command of Captain Isaac Hull. His mission was to be a gun captain on the aft spar deck on the starboard side. He was skilled in using a carronade, shooting a fourteen-pound solid iron round ball.

In the famous battle between the USS *Constitution* and HMS *Guerriere* off the coast of Massachusetts on August 19, 1812, Joshua Crosby of Orleans was aboard *Old Ironsides*. He more than proved his ability as a gun captain. It is said that in the face of withering return fire in a broadside duel, Crosby and his crew kept their cannon trained on the enemy ship's mizzenmast and fired the crucial crippling shot that blasted the mast overboard, leading to the enemy's surrender within a half hour. This smashing sea victory early in the war did much to improve America's sagging morale, giving confidence that our emerging country could compete with other world powers.

A few months later, Crosby again took part when the USS *Constitution* engaged and captured the 38-gun HMS *Java*. When the *Constitution* went into overhaul, Crosby joined Commodore Oliver Hazard Perry on Lake Erie. On September 10, 1813, he took part in a critical battle that helped turn the tide of war in favor of the United States. It was Commodore Perry who hoisted a large defiant banner on the deck of his vessel reading "Don't Give Up the Ship."

The *Lawrence* and *Niagara* were the two ships commended by Perry with Crosby as his gun mate. At first, due to poor securement of the cannon, the *Lawrence* was unable to fire as the battle commenced. Perry jumped aboard a side boat and quickly headed for the *Niagara*. Sailing behind the British man of war, this time with guns aimed by Crosby ready to explode, the British conceded their vulnerability acknowledging defeat. Crosby returned to the USS *Constitution* when she put to sea again in December 1814, slipping the British blockade, taking part in the capture of two more British warships before news arrived that the war had ended.

The USS Constitution *vs.* Gurrierre *oil painting by Anton Fisher. (Courtesy of US Naval Records.)*

After the war, he sailed aboard both overseas and with coastal ships for another two years, concluding as captain of small coasting ships. When he retired from the sea at age sixty, he was appointed keeper of the newly built "Three Sisters" lighthouses, where he continued working for another sixteen years. When the United States began to award military pensions to the military who fought in the War of 1812, he retired again. This time the genteel life of farming called him, working at his home on Tonset Road, Orleans. His home was near the Atlantic, where he spent so much time in his life.

CAPTAIN JOSIAH S. CUMMINGS (1820–1881)
An Ardent Supporter of American Immigration

Josiah Cummings was indeed a descendent of considerable social status. He could trace his family roots back to the Pilgrim Elder Brewster, the source of a village's name, and Governor Thomas Prence. Being associated with so many distinguished Cape Cod gentry, it seems natural that he would find a pathway to a career as a maritime captain. To strengthen his local lineage, he wed Helen Linnell and would become the stepson of Captain Ebenezer Harding Linnell.

Due to his historic connections and familial associations, he possessed a burning passion for ocean life. He commanded the *Clara Wheeler* in the 1840s, gaining a strong reputation as an able coaster. A coaster in those days maintained a routine of trading along the eastern seaboard.

In 1852, he assumed command of the *George Washington*, a ship built for Bramhall and Howe, two well-established commercial shipping magnates. This ship was 210 feet overall and registered in at 1800 tons. In her maiden voyage, she was able to pass the Key West port in under seven days. On the next day, the ship docked in Mobile, Alabama. There, she made the exchange of delivering bales of hay to the South while acquiring a cotton cargo bound for England. On the return voyage from Liverpool, the final set of cargo would be humans, people striving for a new life in a democratic country. This same circuit of cargo and immigrants would repeat itself on several occasions.

During the 1850 to 1860 period, over 2,800,000 immigrants from all corners of the European continent came to the United States. These ocean crossings came with substandard food, overcrowding, and little concern for passenger safety in many cases. However, Captain Cummings always boasted of excellent service and great attention to humane personal detail. His eight hundred passengers openly thanked the captain for their healthy conditions, commendable meals, and personalized service on his first trip. This process was repeated many times over. His newly imported immigrants almost always docked with passengers safe and appreciative of a potential new life. The United States welcomed and valued the work ethic of their new immigrant class.

A shipping record authored by Captain Cummings noted the following restrictions that were embedded within his shipping agreements: "No grog allowed. No passenger food must ever be given to the crew. No profane language is to be heard on the ship, and sheath knives and other weapons are strictly forbidden." These rules, no doubt, contributed mightily to the safety and well-being of his transatlantic cargo.

He also contributed to the American literary scene. In 1842, he agreed to carry the famous English author Charles Dickens from Great Britain to Boston. At first, the famous author became enamored of American life and the vast adulation paid to him by adoring fans. After a while, however, the culture shock of a new country's mores became less appealing to him.

CAPTAIN EBENEZER LINNELL (1811–1864)
Inventor of Sailing Rig Designs

Ebenezer, or Eben to his friends, was born in 1811 in his family home at Barley Neck Road. From a very early age, he always demonstrated a keen interest in all things nautical. His father, Captain Solomon Linnell, a packet owner, was a sea captain before him. As an affable teenager, he secured a post as a cabin boy, learning about the wonders of the sea on a firsthand basis. He worked his way up to first mate and then skipper with smaller packet boats, traveling along the Eastern shore. He fell in love with Rebecca Crosby and had a Cape Cod-style house built for her and his three daughters in 1840.

A transformational moment occurred for him in 1850 when his cargo brought him to Marseilles, France. There he saw a French-designed neo-classical villa that made quite an impression on him. He hired an architect to produce building plans to replicate this house in Orleans. Over the next few years, he also acquired period furniture conducive to a man of wealth from the Orient and Europe. He commissioned his father-in-law, Edmund Crosby, to complete the mansion's construction.

The home, sitting on thirty-five acres, was eventually completed in 1860. The captain was famed for his elegant entertaining within the maritime community. His house was later purchased and eventually restored as a restaurant/banquet hall; The Captain Linnell House was finally opened to the public as a restaurant on Skaket Road.

When not at sea, Captain Linnell demonstrated a strong talent for nautical design. He submitted several United States patents for improved rigging systems. One of his patented marvels fully redesigned the quality of the top sail rig system. It was later added to the schooner of sixty-four new models that vastly improved their speed. Speed was always an important consideration for every captain. A record for speed was established in 1853 when he took command of the *Eagle Wing*

After his fourth day at sea, he experienced a terrific hurricane that would wash two of his men into the brine. Nonetheless, despite several obstacles and bad weather, he managed to make the trip from Boston to San Francisco in a record time of one hundred and five days. Another speed record was noted in a voyage from London to Hong Kong taking him eighty-three days.

His good fortune, however, was not always a positive occurrence. In 1861, he hauled close to two thousand sheep and eighteen shepherds to New Zealand when a storm caused him to crash onto rocky shores. Although his boat was a total loss, the livestock and men were saved. He continued with his journey coming to a new continent through the assistance of a passing rescue vessel.

Once the 1860s arrived, he intended to take leave of his maritime voyages to enjoy his stately new home. He agreed to take one last trip to Brazil. A fierce storm arose during this final voyage while he was still steering the ship. He caught the danger of a spinning boom while the sail was still jibbing, pinning him to the wheel. This freak accident caused him much suffering. He died four days later from these wounds. In 1864,

Artist rendering of Captain Linnell and his wife. (Photo taken at Linnell Inn.)

his wife Rebecca was now widowed, grieving over the loss of her beloved spouse. His intuition was correct. His very last voyage turned out to be one too many.

CAPTAIN JOHN KENDRICK (1740–1795)
Opened the Great Northwest Fur Trade

He was born in 1740 in a home still standing on Route 28 in Orleans. He comes from a strong line of sailing families. His father was Solomon Kenrick (an older spelling), a respected whaler in his day. Kendrick has two distinct facets of his life for which he deserves accolades. During the American Revolution, he was a naval officer and an intrepid explorer opening new trade to the Northwest seas.

As a younger captain, being quite familiar with local inlets and coastlines, he contributed to the infamous Boston Tea Party. He was first commissioned to sail as a privateer for American interests and later as a US Naval Officer as captain of the 18-gun *Fanny*. His ship was one of the first purchased by General George Washington for the Continental Navy.

While stationed in Nova Scotia, he seized a 40-ton schooner, *William*, a West Indies vessel. Later, he captured the English ship *Taunton* about 279 miles outside Antigua. Since this ship was loaded with longboats, it held a valuable commodity for the war effort. His crew continued to demonstrate skill with the captures of smaller ships near Halifax. His luck would finally run out in 1779. He was thrown into British prison. A bit later, he secured release under a prisoner exchange agreement. He later commanded the 16-gun brigantine *Compte d'Estang* and a Rhode Island privateer named the *Marianne* in 1780.

Following the American Revolution, his second career unfolded. He was given control of the *Columbia*, a large trading brigantine. He was forty-seven years old and very knowledgeable about maritime life by this time. With the company of Robert Grey, he assumed the reins of a smaller ship, the *Washington.* Together, they ventured towards the shores of the Northeast coast to engage in the fur trade. Unfortunately, there was always an uneasy antagonism on the part of Grey towards his senior commander.

Kendricks brought his two sons on this journey. John Junior was eighteen years old. He was installed as the fifth mate, while sixteen-year-old Solomon was an ordinary seaman. Their mission was to trade mirrors, beads, tools, and knives with the local natives for sea otter pelts and

The Columbia *in a squall in 1793. Drawing by George Davidson, official ship artist.*

other animal skins. Kendrick quickly learned the native language to gain friendship with the locals, establishing good fluency in record time.

When Grey was found to have struck a fellow seaman, Kendrick ordered him to be held responsible. Grey agreed to disembark and sought a position elsewhere. Grey would later slander and harm the reputation of Kendrick until the very end of his life. Nootka Sound, a region above the state of Washington, became very familiar territory to him. Canadiens renamed the whole region Kendrick Sound.

When Grey first returned to Boston, his lies and mistruths about Kendrick were spread. John Quincy Adams accused Kendrick of "egregious knavery." Although he was vilified for many years, current-day historians have corrected the record, attributing his many heroic deeds as being most beneficial to the United States.

Provincetown

Origin of the Town's Name

Separated from Truro and incorporated in 1727, the name came from a provision in its original charter that reserved title to all lands within Cape Cod to the Province of Massachusetts. The area became a port of call for seafarers and fishermen during the 1600s, and the carousing, drinking, gambling, and smuggling caused the Puritans to nickname the town "Hell Town." Indigenous people called this area "Meeshawn."

A Brief History

The first European to enter this harbor was Giovanni Verrazano, who predated the pilgrims by a full century. He was an Italian explorer hired by the French king in 1524 to find a shorter route to the China Trade. A subsequent European visitor was Bartholomew Gosnold. He was an English explorer commissioned by a British royal monarch to scout through the coastline of North America. His maps indicate the presence of indigenous peoples living in wetus on the Cape Cod coast. They spoke an Algonquin dialect, shared with their closely related sister tribes throughout Cape Cod.

That land, which spanned from Pilgrim Lake, near the present-day border between Provincetown and Truro to Long Point, was claimed officially to benefit the Plymouth Colony. Most original Pilgrims were proud landlubbers, not wishing to make a living from the sea. Nonetheless, in Provincetown, whales were still plentiful and often visited the area coming quite close to the shore. As whales began moving farther out to sea, sailors became more prevalent in Provincetown. Unlike some other parts of the Cape, these men were willing to hunt the large mammals

from afar. By 1737, almost every possible local whaling captain took off
for their hunt approaching the territory of today's Greenland.

Notable Connection to the Sea

Historically, the natural harbor of Provincetown could be called the
cradle of American written law. Pilgrims first landed here in 1620. The
Mayflower seafarers originally intended to land near the Hudson River
but were caught by a windswept storm pushing them to Cape Cod.
Religious separatism was their original goal. The first settlers wished to
find a place free from political or strict religious orthodoxy. Since the
immigrants were settling within a new territory without written laws, a
new written contract was necessary for political clarity. The Mayflower
Compact was finalized on the deck of the *Mayflower* as it lay in the harbor in Provincetown. The wife of Governor Bradford was buried right
here in the port. The major rationale for continuing onto Plymouth was
the joint consensus on the lack of high-quality arable farming land.

Provincetown became the center of the whaling universe in the later
1850s as both Nantucket, and New Bedford declined their efforts. Half
of the professions in town were related to the whaling business. They
were master mariners, mates, navigators, carpenters, crew members, sail
makers, boat builders, riggers, blacksmiths, caulkers, coopers, and chan-
dlers. By the mid-1850s, the schooners owned by many Provincetown
families were sailing to the fertile grounds of the Azores hunting sperm
whales. These ships often returned with more skilled Portuguese seamen
seeking a new start in life. Between 1820 and 1920, more than 160 whaling vessels had been outfitted from Provincetown. This ranking placed
her fifth in overall ships and third in outgoing whaling voyages among
the seventy-two different American whaling ports.

ADMIRAL DONALD BAXTER MACMILLAN (1874–1970)
Explorer and Student of Artic Ice Flows

MacMillan was a noted American explorer, sailor, researcher, and author.
In his career of forty-six years, he made more than thirty expeditions to
the Artic to further advance our basic knowledge of this frozen continent.
His exploits came to the attention of Robert E. Peary, a fellow Bowdoin

College graduate. As a result of saving nine sailors shipwreck at sea, MacMillan's heroic deeds were published in the newspaper, bringing his name to the attention of Peary. Peary invited Macmillan to join him in his 1908 journey to the North Pole. MacMillan traveled more than half of the way through the icy glaciers but finally had to turn back because of frozen heels. Peary was reported as continuing the trip to reach his goal about a month later.

MacMillan spent the next few years conducting ethnological experiments with the Inuit people. As a result of his studies, he gained acclaim as a scholar, demonstrating a knack to master linguistic skills along the way. In 1913, he received a grant from the Natural History Society to lead an expedition to Crocker Land, a territory described by Peary in his research. This trip would turn out to be a disaster in several ways. First, there was never any evidence that the land even existed. Then his ship and crew were stranded on an ice shield for multiple years. He would finally need to be rescued by Captain Robert Bartlett in 1917, who commended the *Neptune*.

In 1918, always the adventurer, he volunteered to serve as an ensign in the Naval Reserve Flying Corps at the age of forty-four years. By the time World War I started, his age would place him among the oldest ensigns ever commissioned by the Navy. Eager to return to the Artic in 1921, he once again raised sufficient funds to quench his intellectual demands. He sailed aboard the *Bowdoin*. This was a ship of his own design, named in honor of his collegiate alma mater. He stayed for over a year conducting several research studies. This trip made history as he kept active communication with the rest of the outside world on his wireless station, the Radio North Pole, during the whole time.

When some scientists theorized that a new ice age was coming in 1925, he once again ventured north to measure what exactly was happening with the Artic ice flows. This trip brought him a new partner in Richard E. Byrd. Unfortunately, many of his aerial photographs were not scientifically useful due to the quality used in the extremes of inclement weather. Nonetheless, the experience was positive for Byrd as he learned more about the Artic terrain, mastering the more modern navy meteorological equipment. The next year, he successfully reached the first documentable voyage to the center of the North Pole.

Admiral James MacMillan aboard his ship, the Bowdoin.
(Courtesy of US Naval Records.)

His reputation for service to the country became legendary. When World War II broke out in his mid-sixties, he again left his retirement to fight with his ship, the *Bowdoin*. The town of Provincetown celebrated their local hero by naming the town's major pier in his honor. At ninety-five, he died in Provincetown, not very far from that very pier bearing his name.

COLLINS STEVENSON (1847–1904)
A Black Whaling Captain

Before abolishing slavery in the United States, black people were denied the right to work in most professions. Even if they made any income, the money had to be paid directly to their owner. One clear exception to this rule would be the whaling industry. Although not completely color-blind, what mattered the most to the owners of the whaling ships was the sailor's personal ability to handle a sail, toss a harpoon, and work tirelessly on a voyage filled with many dangerous aspects. Whaling was an egalitarian trade that welcomed people of every race, ethnicity, color, and background.

In the 1700s, indigenous tribe members from the Wampanoags and the Aquinnah comprised most of a whaling crew. European whaling captains typically gave the commands and acquired larger shares of wealth. In the 1800s, black sailors comprised at least one-third of the whaling contingency. Their share of the financial bottom line often was equitably distributed to the whole crew. Throughout the early nineteenth century, whaling, especially the demand for whale oil, continued to be the third-largest business in Massachusetts and the fifth most profitable business in the country.

Captain Collins Stevenson was a well-established black whaler. He was born in 1847 in St. Vincent in the West Indies. He came to America at the age of eighteen. As a youth, he volunteered enthusiastically as an ordinary sailor, slowly but surely mastering the necessary steps to reach the status of a master sailor. He became a shipmaster of the *Carrie D. Knowles* at forty-two. When several whaling captains would engage in only a few whaling voyages throughout their career, records indicate that he engaged in at least eighteen different trips.

Immediately after the Civil War, seven black whaling captains were sailing out of Provincetown. One of the principal owners of whaling ships, including the *Carrie D. Knowles*, was also black, George A. Knowles. During his tenure as a captain, he brought in whale oil valued today at a rate of $3.1 million. An interesting footnote is that none of the Provincetown whalers were initially born into slavery. They were freemen who fought for the privilege to work on a fishing boat on an even basis with other seamen. Stevenson's wealth allowed him to rise to a lead mason in the King Hiram's Lodge.

In January 1904, Stevenson ventured out on a whaling expedition with a crew of twelve sailors, and there is still a shrouded of mystery as to what happened. His typical fishing trips would last approximately twenty days. There were three basic theories as to how the trip might have ended.

At first thought, it could have been a terrible storm at sea or as a second choice perhaps a ferocious whale capsized the boat. A third potential theory also emerged. An American seaman claimed that this crew was held prisoner in a Venezuelan prison. Senator Henry Cabot Lodge examined this story but could not reach a firm conclusion. It was either a cruel hoax or possibly a true story. One sad consequence to this representation was that his wife, Hannah, had definitive plans to remarry. Once she had learned even of the remote possibility that her husband may not have been lost at sea and is still alive., she decided to remain unwed. However, Captain Knowles never returned from his trip, nor did she ever remarry.

NATHANIEL ATWOOD (1807–1886)
A World-Famous Ichthyologist

In Atwood's remarkable life, he served as a scholar, a fisherman, a naturalist, a state senator, a comparative zoologist, and a co-founder of the Ichthyologist Department of Massachusetts Institute of Technology. An ichthyologist is a marine biologist focusing on fish classified as bony or cartilaginous. It is a study of their history, behavior, reproductive habits, and growth patterns. Coming from a long line of devoted fishermen, he dedicated his life to a formal study of this specific sea life.

He was raised as a fisherman living on seasonal catches of sea-herring, mackerel cod, and other scaled fish as a youth. His family was the first to reside at Long Point in his early life.

He was intensely interested in examining the habits of fish species. Initially not knowing exactly how to approach scientific research, he detailed his findings as a fishing captain with copious notes. His keen observations on fishing patterns would be welcomed into the Massachusetts State Senate in later life. He provided local talks for Provincetown fishermen, which were finally memorialized in a series of lectures known as the Atwood Collection.

His life was spent roaming the seas for five decades. On one occasion, as a captain of the whaler, the *Cetacean*, he came upon a British ship named the *Lone Star*, sinking rapidly. Nine crew members and a dog were facing a near-certain death by drowning. His heroic efforts saved the day with a dramatic rescue. The queen was so impressed with his work that she awarded him an engraved telescope eventually donated to the town's historical collection.

As a scientist, he observed fishing patterns that were beneficial to the industry. His enthusiasm for cod liver oil as a medicinal benefit would be substantiated by other future researchers. His research work led to a newly identified species of shark. The scientific community honored him by naming it *Charchariae Atwoodii* to memorialize his name.

His collaboration with famed biologist Louis Agassiz would later lead to a series of lectures in 1868, which became foundational to this area of study. His hometown demonstrated respect for him

Nathanial Atwood, world-class Icyologist

by establishing the Atwood Wharf. A eulogist in 1886 proclaimed him a man of "serene temper and intelligence whose existence was characterized by service, public spirit, and intellectualism." He is particularly known for his contributions to ichthyological classification, including extinct species such as the megalodon, and the study of geological history, including the founding of glaciology.

LUCINDA ROSE (1890–1973)
A Daughter's View of her Azorean's Father Life as a Fisherman

As a commemorative project, in 1971, the Provincetown Historical Association decided to interview selected people who had a story to share with their community. A historian named Nell Husted sat down with a woman who had seen significant changes in her life. Lucinda Rose had lived in Provincetown for over ninety years. She saw Teddy Roosevelt lay the Pilgrim Monument cornerstone. She also witnessed dramatic cultural shifts within her sleepy seaside town. She observed that from 1870 to 1895, Provincetown had the largest overall population on the Cape. The harbors, wharves, and docks were constantly abuzz with fishing, whaling, and commercial expeditions.

The demographics of the day reflected the fact that many new settlers comingled with the inherent New England heritage. Three large groups of immigrants arrived from the Azores, Eastern Nova Scotia (originally from Scotland), and many Irish. Town records indicate that over seventy-five percent of all shipping crews were made up of newly arrived immigrants. Her father, Joao, was a proud Cape Verdean.

Even from her earliest years, she was aware of her heritage and inter-racial roots. Her bloodline included African slave background, European heritage, and even Middle East lineage. Her exotic physical beauty was always shining through during her existence.

Joao made the trip from Cape Verde to Cape Cod in 1876. With the official outlawing of the Slave Trade, a young Joao saw that vast changes were coming to Cape Verde. His island was a holding place for slaves taken from Africa. Brava, a Cape Verde Island, was losing prosperity in several different ways. He decided that coming to the New World was the best way to advance to a better life. One day, when a New Bedford whaler came to the Azores, he agreed to serve two years before the mast in exchange for passage to the new continent.

His first job was to serve as a cook aboard a fleet of fishing boats combing the waters of the Grand Banks. When he was aboard a whaler, the captain, the first mate, the cooks, and the cabin boy stayed on the boat while the remaining sailors faced the elements by harpooning and dragging the whale to the ship's side.

After living in a boarding house for some years, he saved enough funds to buy a small house. By the end of that decade, he invited his wife to join him. Lucinda's mother was the daughter of a Cape Verdean surgeon. Her constant fear of a seismic volcano eruption within her hometown remained etched in her mind. Without hesitation, she gladly left Brava to come to a new cape, Cape Cod. The two places had much in common. The ever-present soil erosion and large stretches of open beach were strikingly similar. Her trip of 3,000 miles took sixty days.

At home, the children were expected to speak both English and Crioulo, a Cape Verdean creole dialect. While her father would be out at sea often for three months at a time, the children were expected to gather berries, cherries, and beach plums. Then, they were asked to barter their local fruits for other needed commodities at the local store. She saw her parents as a loving couple, but she did not have the same good fortune. Her first husband was lost at sea after three years of her marriage at nineteen. Her second marriage turned out to be a "horrendous mismatch" and did not endure. She happily spent her final days in the Cape End Manor in Provincetown.

VIOLA FISH COOK (1855–1922)
Wife of John Cook; The Frigid Queen of Provincetown

At the age of twenty-two, Viola accepted the marriage proposal of John Atkins Cook. He was several years her junior, but she deemed her union to be a good one. John had the official reputation of being called the Ice King. He would boast how the coldness of the Artic did not intimidate him whatsoever. His whaling trips would require long periods of winter harshness.

During her final days, living in Provincetown, the wife had the reputation of being a frightful unbalanced woman who would he heard sharpening her kitchen knives at all hours of the day and night. Her personality even presented itself as a framework for a character within a Eugene O'Neil play.

In 1893, she took her first whaling trip aboard the *Narvarch*. It was the custom of certain whalers to spend their full winter in the artic sea so that when the first signs of Spring woold arrive, their harpoons would be ready. She passed many a day that winter in socializing and playing cards with the wives of four other captains, all coming from a similar situation. For John, it was fun but only was seen as acceptable to her. In 1898, she made her second trip with her daughter Emma. This voyage was slightly more enjoyable as she was able to see a new ship picked up in Sweden, bringing her daughter along for company. Playing and teaching the piano helped her to pass the time.

In 1901, she went again to the Arctic. The captain threatened to leave her if she chose not to accompany him this time. She eventually relented to the demand. The harshness of the winter months was immense as she spent 58 days in almost full darkness with very little company. Eventually the crew considered mutiny. The captain's wife stayed in her cabin, listening with trepidation to the loud uproar springing up around her. Captain Cook realized the extent of her misery. In his log, he said: "She was prostrated by grief and sank into a deep state of melancholia." In 1906, the captain employed a new scheme to entice her to make still another journey. He christened his new ship *Viola* using her name in her memory. With this almost twisted gesture, she felt obligated to go once again. This time she contracted beriberi with her mental and physical health suffering. She returned to Provincetown, a broken woman.

Upon her return, the captain feared for his very life as his wife's mental health was precarious. He would bolt his door closed at night to avoid a possible knife thrust at him. He would eventually leave her, deciding to marry a much younger woman. Viola died feeling alone and abandoned. At that point, the town took pity upon her treated her husband, the captain, as a "Persona Non-Grata" in the Provincetown community.

The husband documented his frequent Arctic adventures in a book titled *Pursuit of the Whale*, in which he boasts of his courageous approach to the whaling industry.

The Viola *whaling ship at dock. (Courtesy of Digital Commonwealth, New Bedford Public Library.)*

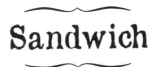

Sandwich

Origin of the Town's Name

The town is named in honor of Sandwich in Kent, England, which was the English hometown of John Humphrey. Humphrey served as the first Assistant Governor of the Massachusetts Bay Colony. Humphrey, himself, in 1637, encouraged the move of sixty families from Saugus to come down to their new residence on the Cape Cod Bay. The region was incorporated in 1639, and it is the oldest town on Cape Cod, as deemed by the historical record. The villages of Sandwich include East Sandwich, Scorton Neck, Farmersville, Forestdale, and Wakeby.

A Brief History

Sandwich was initially occupied by the Algonquian-speaking Wampanoags, who assisted the Pilgrims of Plymouth Colony. It was settled in 1637 by a group from Saugus (today's Lynn) with full permission granted by the Pilgrim Colony.

Sandwich was the site of an early Quaker settlement, today hosting the oldest continuous Quaker Meeting House in the United States. As conflicts emerged for supremacy with other religious groups, some Quakers left the town for further settlements elsewhere, such as Dartmouth, Massachusetts. Many of the current Sandwich families can trace their heritage back to Quaker lineage.

The earliest industry revolved around agriculture, with fishing and trading also providing financial relief for the town. Later, the town grew into a small industrial mecca along the Scusset River and Old Harbor Creek and its tributaries. A major contributor to Sandwich's growth would be Deming Jarves. He founded the Boston and Sandwich Glass

Factory in 1825. Since Sandwich had proximity to a shallow harbor as a possible canal site, it could easily gather local timber supplies to fuel the glass furnaces. Lead glass became very popular in early America with multiple colors and endurance.

CAPTAIN JOSIAH ELLIS (1789–1829)
Saved by an Act of Good Providence

Even though Sandwich was not significantly known for large ships or long ocean voyages, it was known for being practical. There were several shorter safe maritime runs that the sandwich sailors would undertake. Since the demand for heating fuel in Boston was high, particularly in the winter and the cape in its early days, a natural new business unfolded the need for a healthy supply of wood. Captain Ellis had a regular route of delivering lumber to the port of Boston

His ship, the *Almira*, began an eventful yet tragic voyage in January 1826. The crew was three men, yet only one managed to survive. In addition to the captain, his son Josiah and a seaman named John Smith were on board. The ship was close to reaching Boston Harbor. A bitter cold Northeaster sprang up, catching the seamen off-guard. The winds whipped so strongly that even their best efforts to remain stationary or reach port were blocked. The captain lost all means of control of his ship. They buffeted in the storm for hours, with fierce winds whipping around in the bay. Although they could almost visually see the town of Plymouth at one point, they suddenly were blown in the opposite direction from where they were heading to the southeast deeper into the bay. Their mainmast became fully iced. Their other sails were also covered by ice and could not be unfurled. During the blizzard, all sails snapped off, hurling into the bitter cold.

Quickly, the three men were covered by the ocean waves, rapidly changing the whole boat into a sheet of ice. Their clothes became menacing torture as their bodies were now one large stick of frost. They attempted to go into the ship's hold, but the ship listed badly. The crew knew it was unsafe to remain there. The waves swelled to such a degree that on several occasions, the waves engulfed the entire vessel, with the men clinging on for dear life. As best they thought that they could attempt to remain on the deck facing the rime and cold winds, their ship flew like a loose kite would do on a windy day all through the night

Realizing the urgency, there was an attempt by local townspeople who became aware of their predicament to save them. Volunteers from the town of Dennis rowed out in a smaller boat and cried out, offering verbal support. It was simply impossible for the rescuers to get too close to the vessel as it merged into an icy block. Seaman John Smith realized that his time was perhaps ended.

John crept up the windlass, a large mechanism used for hauling larger cargo. Within ten minutes, he froze to death. As the other helpless volunteers watched, they saw the captain become the next victim. He, too, attempted to get to the vessel's side, but he also met his demise in the frosty elements. As luck would have it, a large wave appeared once again and rocked the boat past the Dennis breakers unto the beach. The rescuers arrived to save the young Josiah in the nick of time. He was immediately wrapped up in warm woolen blankets and was thawed back to better health within a warm fireplace in Dennis.

Showing great determination and a strong New England spirit, the younger Josiah got up the courage to purchase a new vessel and, within a few years, continued his father's work. He, too, became a wood pile carrier attending to the needs of the Boston homeowners. The deadly New England storms would once again claim the lives of many a mariner, but Josiah was spared from any future catastrophe.

CAPTAIN EZRA NYE (1798–1866)
A Brilliant Mariner and Entrepreneur

This captain was proclaimed by an author no less distinguished than Henry Kittridge as being the "most celebrated shipmaster that Sandwich ever produced." As a young captain, he drove the clipper *Amethyst* westward from Liverpool to Boston in the remarkable time of 20 days. His maritime reputation was so distinguished that when a new luxury ship, the *Independence*, was built, there was little debate as to whom should be the master.

The Independence was among the largest new packet boats operated by the Swallow Tail Shipping Line out of New York. It stood at 140

feet in length. One of the honors accorded to this ship was carrying the United States President's mail directly to London. On one of the shortest timed runs for its day, the captain sailed from New York to Liverpool in only 34 days, with the eastward direction only taking 14 days to cross the Atlantic. This time is further proof of his skill, as his cross-Atlantic voyage took only one day more than the one accomplished by Asa Eldridge. His trip was accomplished with a ship that was 120 feet shorter in size and lighter in tonnage.

Captain Nye kept command of the *Independence* throughout the 1830s. Realizing that his services were more and more in demand, he left the big home built in Sandwich and moved to Baltimore to be nearer to his clipper ships. His skill became a national talking point. In 1845, the *Henry Clay* was launched as one of the biggest merchant ships of the era. Nye was given command of her maiden voyage. In 1846, a terrific storm brought him to crash-land before the New York port and was washed ashore in New Jersey, losing six men in the experience,

Even the lord of British royalty extolled his skill. Lord William Lennox traveled to Liverpool aboard the *Henry Clay*. He once wrote: "The accommodations afforded to me on this magnificent ship were superior to any other sailing vessel that I ever saw."

Known for his outstanding propriety and grace, he once rescued the entire crew of a British bark as the ship was beginning to disintegrate into pieces. For his efforts, Queen Victoria rewarded his efforts with a medal.

The Pacific, *a steamer captained by Ezra Nye.*

To further demonstrate his civility, when a famous American actress was tardy in her booking to secure a private stateroom, he offered her his private accommodations. He simply moved to a smaller room himself. Upon retirement, he never forgot his relatives in Sandwich. He would often send them best wishes and actual financial support to those in need.

Later in his career, he decided to take a turn with the steamer ships. E.K. Collins has started his steam packet line challenging the British Curanderos Line. He took the steamer, the *Pacific*, across the sea in only nine days, which became the first trans-Atlantic ship to do so in under ten days.

NATHANIEL BURGESS (1812–1891)
Understood the Perils of the Artic Ocean

Nathaniel came from a family of sturdy fishermen. He was born in what is known today as Pocasset, a village in Sandwich. His wife, Anne, also loved the sea and had no qualms to bring their two children on multiple year-long voyages. As a whaler captain, he realized his desire to chase this large mammal. It would bring him far away from Cape Cod. It became most obvious that whales were more plentiful in the Artic regions. To arrive at this destination, ships had to traverse down to the South America tip to sail around the Cape of Good Horn to reach past the Pacific Ocean.

His ship became entrapped within an Arctic ice flow in one of his voyages. The captain was extremely anxious that fresh water would run out. He sent out a scouting party to walk on icy banks to see if any freshwater reservoir could be discovered. Luck was certainly on his side. His crew was able to identify a water source. After a long march, a water source was found within a considerable distance from the ship. The men bottled what they found to retrieve it back to the crew.

At one point, his logbook notes that he was trapped deep in the ice for twelve days, stationary with minimal supplies. During that time, his children found a new ice-filled wonderland to play in while the crew made multiple trips over frigid conditions to secure one hundred barrels of water. Other crew members picked and pried the ice to set the vessel free. On another trip, he uncovered a young stowaway, George Bauldry, whom he would eventually adopt and train as a sea captain. His adopted son would be recognized as one of the most adroit sailors in that period.

He continued his whaling career for eighteen years, earning him a solid reputation as a skillful mariner and a wealthy businessman. There was no doubt in his mind that whaling was a most perilous way to make a living. A quote attributed by him in his last whaling trip focused on the crew's ever-present condition. "Discipline is of the utmost importance. When you have men from nine different nationalities, the elemental goal is far from forming tight bonding connections. To avoid their mutiny, you must be alert."

He retired from whaling at forty-two and entered a new and safer endeavor as an oyster farmer. He grew this enterprise with skill and dedication, leaving his two sons an industry they could further cultivate and grow. His legacy of integrity and charity towards others remained a model for his sons to emulate.

PELEG NYE (1817–1896)
A Modern Day Jonah in The Whale Story

Peleg was the seventh and final child born to Heman and Mehitable Nye of Sandwich. His mother was a direct descendant of the *Mayflower's* John Howland, born in 1817. His dad was an established coaster, delivering and securing merchandise along the Eastern shores. In 1834, he was a green whaler but would become a veteran sailor over the next twenty years.

In 1835, at the age of seventeen, Peleg and his older brother, Josiah Fish Nye, made their way to New Bedford, which had become the successor to Nantucket as the whaling capital of the world. Due to the British blockades during the war of 1812, a new mainland port was needed to transact its business. No doubt, he would have journeyed to port via a scheduled packet boat run from Sandwich to the new harbor.

On his first whaling adventure, he was hired as an able body seaman aboard the *India*, leaving for a 2,220-mile excursion to Brisbane, Australia. The captain for that run was Joshua Coffin of the well-established Nantucket Coffin family. During the first six months at sea, the ship had already taken seven smaller-sized whales. This voyage was his first excursion around the Cape Horn. The ship log recalls that Peleg was able to attend to a broken rudder and replaced it in a manner that transformed it to "performing very well."

Most of his next whaling adventures initiated from the Provincetown Harbor. At this point, New Bedford had much larger boats with heavier tonnage prepared to travel to the Pacifica and up to the Arctic Circle. Typically, Provincetown departing whalers used smaller capacity boats, staying closer to the shore with frequent returns to land for the evening.

In 1864, he had an experience with a sperm whale that seemed reminiscent of a biblical passage. After being at sea for nine months, the *George W Lewis* had but little whale oil in its hold. As the first mate, it was his responsibility to fire an explosive lance into a harpooned whale.

Things changed abruptly when the ship turned from the Porgus Bank near the Cape Verdean Island of Sal. A large sperm whale suddenly was spotted on the horizon; Nye leaped to the task, quickly becoming the boat steerer to approach the maritime giant. The ship log read: "The whale immediately began sounding and ran out 100 fathoms of line from the three hundred feet they had available." The ocean's waves crashed with might and became rough. It appeared as if the whale might break the line. The log stated, "Quick as a flash, the whale threw his head around as the pursuit boat banged into the body of the whale. The waves crashing wildly, dropping Peleg to its side and directly into the open mouth of the whale."

The upper teeth of the whale are soft, serving only as a type of strainer. Fortunately for Nye, his legs fit into the spaces between the teeth and their sockets. As the whale started to soften his frame to the constant physical attack, Nye gasped for air as his lungs became filled with water rendering him unconscious.

He was under the sea for such a long time that the crew was certain that his demise was imminent. However, his body did eventually surface at the ocean's top. He was brought up on deck. Captain Holmes had a rudimentary knowledge of medical knowledge. Nye's body needed immediate surgery. His treatment lasted for eight hours, and there was but slight hope of recovery. Four days later, in intense pain, Nye became expressive, telling his peers, "I came as close as slipping the cable as any man ever did and still live.to describe it."

Both Peleg Nye and the biblical figure of Jonah have the same claim "We then prayed unto the Lord and came out of the fish's belly. I was delivered." He would continue his whaling adventures to become captain of his own vessel. He retired at the age of 62 and was listed in the town's register as a retired mariner. On August 11, *The Boston Daily Advisor* mentioned the funeral of Capt. Peleg Nye which was held in Hyannisport. He was cited as being well known for being swallowed whole by a whale.

CAPTAIN ROLAND GIBBS (1806–1867)
Skipper of the Acorn

In 1825, Deming Jarves arrived in Sandwich with a vision to use some of the natural sand in Sandwich to make glass. The Boston & Sandwich Glass Company (B&S) was started. The influence on the town was immense, converting it from a rural community to an industrial site. His vision provided new employment and expanded tax revenue resulting in several town improvements. Sandwich was where the glass was made, with Boston being the distribution hub. The B&S produced thousands of pounds of glassware per week, transporting their output via small packet sailing ships.

Things changed a bit when the newly formed Cape Cod Branch Railroad came to town in 1848. The railroad expressed a desire to haul the valuable glass shipment to Boston. However, Deming Jarves felt the railroad fees were exorbitant. He fought the railroad executives, threatening to use his large ship to move inventory. Local legend states the head of the railroad. General Agent Sylvanus Bourne was dismissive of this claim, scornfully saying: "The acorn has not yet been planted that will grow the timber for that vessel."

Jarves never believed in the power of idle threats. In 1853, he ordered the construction of a ship with both steam and sail to be delivered to Sandwich. Its captain would be Roland Gibbs from Sandwich. When it steamed into Sandwich Harbor, people could see the implied irony within its name, the *Acorn*. He struck a note of pure revenge by calling it by that name. As a matter of coincidence, the acorn with oak leaf cluster was also one of the firm's favorite themes for decorating glassware.

The *Acorn* made two round trips per week to Boston taking freight and passengers. Not surprisingly, the *Acorn* was never profitable. After Jarves left the company in 1859, the directors completed a successful contract with the railroad with all freight from the glass factory to be taken to Boston by rail. Without a need for the *Acorn*, it was sold. For approximately four years, the ship served as a steamer running the Provincetown/Boston route taking a five-hour journey. Capt. Gibbs continued to command the vessel. By 1862, the *Acorn* ended up as a ship used by the Union Navy during the Civil War. In a sad ending, it was sunk by Confederate forces off the coast of the Carolinas.

Sandwich Glass Company.

Truro

Origin of the Town's Name

Its name comes from a suggestion of Thomas Paine Jr. (who, by the way, is no relation to the author of *Common Sense*). He was a local land speculator who acquired a large parcel of lots, calling his enterprise the Pamet Proprietors. He, himself, came from Truro, England. In his opinion, he found the views of the beach to be very similar in contour and emotional feeling to his homeland. The English version of Truro derived from a Cornish term signifying the "concordance of three rivers."

A Brief History

Truro was settled by English immigrants in the 1690s situated in the northernmost portion of the town of Eastham. The town was officially separated from Eastham and incorporated as a separate town in 1709. Fishing, whaling, and shipbuilding comprised the town›s early industry. Due to its proximity to the sea and only being a tiny narrow strip of land, with the Atlantic Ocean to its right and Cape Cod Bay to the left, it was obvious that its industry would be mostly maritime. These operations were forced to shift to other locations when the harsh tides of the Lower Cape began decimating the town's main port during the 1850s. It seemed easier to move a business site to a new spot that was better protected and had a greater land mass than to stay put.

Today much of the land mass is incorporated into protected the National Seashore Trust. In the late 19th and early 20th century, Truro was always a popular location for people who loved the natural beauty. Due to the quality and texture of its light source, sunrises and sunsets are special events in this region. It attracted the attention of many an artist such as Edward Hopper.

A Notable Connection to the Sea

An important part of the Pilgrim journey can be traced to the town of Truro. When the pilgrims landed at the Provincetown harbor, they sent out scouting boats to test the fertility of the land. Governor Bradford and some other hearty souls traversed through the thickly settled lands at the Head of the Meadows Beach. They indeed found fresh drinking water that they carried back to the ship. Nonetheless, they found the land too sandy and perhaps not suitable enough for farming.

There was an abundance of potential grain to be cultivated, yet the narrowness of this stretch of land was also disappointing. Shortly after this brief trip through the forest, a decision was made to stay as a group nearer to the tip of the Cape for the winter and then proceed a few months later to Plymouth for the site of their new colony. Its site can be deemed as the birthplace of the Coast Guard as in 1915 President Wilson merged the Life Saving Stations of Truro with the Revenue Cutting Service to form a new military branch.

CAPTAIN EDWIN KNIGHT COLLINS (1802–1878)
The World Class Shipping Magnet

Leaving his hometown of Truro at the age of fifteen, Edward desired to see the vast world made available through sea travel. He shipped out from Truro only to be captured by a British blockade runner during the War of 1812. Following that experience, he started to sail to Mexico, introducing a host of new products to the eastern shores. He eventually developed a fleet of ships so powerful that he could take on the competition of the Cunard Line. A prudent tactical decision was made to transplant older sailing vessels for more modern wooden side-wheelers steam packets which could carry United States Mail and passengers across the Atlantic to Europe.

He would become one of the best-known men of the sea when sailing was at the center of American enterprise. After leaving the cape in 1818,

Collins began work as a shipping clerk for his father, Captain Israel Collins, another Truro man, starting his own firm as a shipping merchant in New York City. When his father died in 1832, Edward took over the company's reins, expanding it considerably.

In 1854, 233 passengers were aboard the ship, the *Artic*. The list included his wife, his nineteen-year-old daughter, and his son, Henry Colt. The ship encountered great fog once they neared the coast of Newfoundland. Another smaller ship with a propeller cutting into the deck. Edward persevered in running the firm.

Several years later, Collins built four passenger vessels and started the Dramatic Shipping Line. Its name for the company was chosen as it derives from the personalities of many celebrated American actors. In 1840, Collins chose his uncle, John Collins, to become skipper of the *Roscius*, the largest US shipping vessel ever to navigate waters at that time. John Collins was already the captain of the firm's oldest vessel, the *Shakespeare* (please note how the name was spelled in this manner on the ship's side).

Wreck of the Artic *by James Buttersworth. (Courtesy of Library of Congress.)*

BENJAMIN RICH (1775–1851)
A Champion for the U S Coastguard Service

For fifty years, he sailed the deep ocean waters aboard the *Oxnard*, prominently known for his ferocious courage. In May 1818, the packet *Canton* blew up within its local harbor. Captain Rich was the first to jump out from the dock to rescue the crew, utterly heedless of another imminent explosion. It was believed that he saved the lives of over ten sailors.

In 1841, when eight different fishing vessels were lost at sea during a range of dire storms, Captain Rich quickly gathered some subscription papers among the various merchants of Boston to obtain six thousand dollars for the distressed widows and orphans. He served as President of the Humane Society of Massachusetts, a charitable organization dispensing funds to only the neediest of people.

There was also a need for additional safe shelters or huts to be built near the shores of Truro. This requirement was reinforced with the observation of the wreck of *the Brutus*. This disaster saw the death of twenty crew members directly off the coast of Truro. When the sailor's shivering bodies were snatched from the ocean, there was no safe place to warm them up from the snowstorm taking place around them. The irony is that a small improperly built shelter already existed nearby, yet it was in such poor shape as to render it ineffective.

Truro's first set of huts were the six that the Humane Society would initially construct between Race Point and Chatham. They stood on wooden piles and were eight-foot square. Working with Reverend James Freeman, a petition was sent to the federal government in 1790 pleading for consideration for planning a desperately needed lighthouse, lifesaving stations, and safety huts along the edge of the ocean. Truro was indeed deemed a most dangerous shoreline for marine wrecks and navigation among dangerous shoals.

The original type of light designed for a lighthouse was called an "eclipser." As used in the original lighthouse, it was quite primitive and not sufficient for public society. The light came from spider lamps which were nothing more than a few pans of whale oil containing wicks but had no chimneys to release the smoke. The smoke would smudge the glass panels and thus render the vision blocked. Rich saw the inadequacy of these rough initial attempts to save sailors but persisted in fighting for federal and local funds to benefit injured mariners and widows and upgrade the necessary safety stations and functional lighthouses to minimize ship-wrecked disasters.

In a very true sense, he was a champion for a U.S. Coast Guard system personally overseeing the construction of eighteen life-saving huts along the coastal shores from Provincetown to Chatham. A letter of appreciation drafted by the Humane Society cites, "You have been instrumental in providing for the wants and relief of so many ship-wrecked mariners. In an hour of grave storm, you have shown the way." Unfortunately, these huts were often kept in poor repair and lacked blankets and clean straw for warmth. He died upon the steep hilltop just to the northeast of Ebenezer Freeman's home, where he also was buried alongside his family members.

CAPTAIN HENRY ATKINS (1700–1774)
A Merchant for the Indigenous People of Labrador

Truro has a strong reputation for being a pioneering adventurous community. A fine example of this pioneer spirit can be found in Captain Henry Atkins. He started his whaling exploits as early as 1720. He started his business in much the same way that whalers out of Nantucket started to pursue the whale as a revenue stream. Contrary to popular belief, the fortunes of the early whalers were very difficult to acquire,

There was a need for financial supporters to embark upon long sea voyages lasting twelve to sixteen months in most cases. Once in debt, the whaling captain had to have successful voyages to pay off the acquired interest and support. It took equal skill and good fortune to make a comfortable living in this competitive trade. His ship, appropriately called the *Whale*, would serve him well.

In 1729, he took his ship from Boston to the Davis Strait, separating Greenland from the Baffin Island, not far from the Arctic Circle. Going this far North distinguished his open ocean experience from the Nantucket sailors who originally stayed much closer to the New England

Coast. On his return trip., he was able to negotiate trade routes along the coast of Labrador with the native American and Canadian tribes. He would return thirty years later to these same ports. The natives were more than willing to trade beaver furs, forest timber, and other local produce.

On one of his trips to the Davis Strait, he captured a polar bear cub and brought it back to the colonies. This was the first time the early colonists saw such an impressive creature. He acclaimed fame by bringing the animal to Boston Harbor. He would produce a show, providing a verbal narrative on how the ferocious mother would guard her children against any undue harm.

His trapping strategies were discussed in detail. His route to Greenland was eventually followed by other whalers in Nantucket, New Bedford, and Provincetown. As the species diminished, the locality of the whale needed a greater arena of pursuit. He was a student of scientific data, often taking notes on how and where the sperm whale lived and functioned. He was often cited in research papers delivered to the Royal Society in London. Atkins described the ingredients in the substance of ambergris and how it is extracted from the bowels of a sperm whale. Ambergris is used as a perfume base. It became a very valuable commodity fetching a good profit in many ports.

In his later years, he witnessed the pleasant sight of many whales approaching the Provincetown harbor. In 1760, a diary from another sea captain also noted the presence of many whales in the vicinity of Provincetown while citing Captain Atkins as the kindly father bidding them all welcome.

CAPTAIN RICHARD JAMES (1757–1831)
Revolutionary War Hero Who Captured a British Ship

In 1777, during the American Revolution, an American seaman captured a British man-of-war with but a single small cannon and without firing a single shot. The British seized the *Compte d'Estaing*, an American brig anchored off the coast of Truro. The American captain and his crew came ashore when the ship was beached, avoiding destruction. Not being sure exactly what his first step might be, Captain James could get a message sent out first to Truro and then back to Boston Harbor to a ship commander, asking for the next steps.

He was proud that his militia crew was still intact. He stated that the Truro men mustered early in the morning but could not repel the superior British forces. He could escape and secured a small cannon, bringing it to an adjacent hill. They aimed the weapon at the British boarding party from the top of a high hill. The captain saw a chance to reboard his former ship with his men at high tide.

He stated that he quickly unloaded canvas, powder, and small arms. He stored these defensive weapons around the town, entrusting them to the local militia. He has requested permission to unload the ship's entire cargo. He had about six hundred bushels of salt brought from the West Indies. American merchants requested this cargo. It was acknowledged that salt was greatly needed for the war effort. Any expense at reshipping now would prove too costly.

The authorities in Boston directed him to transfer the cargo to a sloop sent out from Boson Harbor. After cargo transfer, the British lost all interest in the deserted brig lying on the beach. The American military provided the captain with two more field cannons, cannonballs, and gun powder a few days later. These provisions were delivered for two different reasons. First, it would provide annoyance to the enemies, and secondly, it would provide supplemental safety for those brave men who were still being threatened with the British man-of-war.

The two additional cannons brought the total number to four. These cannons were small, only able to shoot two three-pound balls at a time. A crew of thirty men was now enlisted at Truro, and town meeting records stated that additional officers were selected for the prospect of additional conflict.

There is no record of these cannons ever being used. Despite their lack of use, these instruments came in very handy when the British man-of-war, the *Somerset*, was beached near Provincetown while chasing an American schooner. By seeing the various cannons, the British feared for their boat and surrendered. The capture of this vessel secured a tremendous note of accomplishment for the American cause. As the newly established blockade wreaked havoc with colonial shipping, he could take credit for the capture of 460 British sailors in one momentous event.

ISAAC SMALL (1840–1892)
Member of the United States Life Saving Service

Isaac Small was a marine agent of the United States Life Saving Service in 1880. Members led a very difficult and often thankless life at the ocean's edge facing constant danger. These men realized how underpaid they were. Money was not usually their guiding aspiration. Beachcombers of wrecked ships often were paid by the same source.

They were paid by insurance underwriters or ship owners commissioned to salvage as much gear and freight as possible. Initial qualifications for a maritime agent would be a strong local knowledge of the cape's shoals and complete courage to deal with oceanic storms. These men earned as little as five dollars per day when an average salary in this era would have been at least fifteen dollars per week.

The Life Saving Agents were paid a total of sixty-five dollars per month. In addition, if any injury would occur, they would be removed from service, losing any hope of an ultimate government pension. Worse yet, if the agents were killed on duty, their families never received additional financial support or even recognition for their valiant work.

Their typical day would consist of lifeboat drills, setting up breech buoys, and spending endless hours maintaining constant surveillance of ships troubled at sea. Their busiest employment period began in November and could last well into May or beyond. Their motto bordered on the edge of fatalistic philosophy as they would sing and chant, "You have to go out to sea, but you don't necessarily have to come back."

Considering the dangers inherent in their tasks and the physical strength needed to do their work, Isaac Small worked an amazing number of years. Starting his duties in 1861, he worked for thirty years. To cite just one concrete example of heroism, let us examine what happened at the Peaked Hill Bars Station in 1880.

Eight men were called to duty on a cold winter night that winter when violent waves threatened the *Trumbell*. The first boat of the Life Savers was manned with a crew of four. They rowed out to rescue the crew. They braved the elements without the benefit of moonlight or even a workable lantern.

They approached the ship as close as they possibly could get but then decided if they pulled too close alongside in their dory, ferocious waves from the oceanside might splinter their vessel. Not having the option of a breech buoy, they encouraged the crew to jump individually into the freezing wintery waters so that they could be taken to the safety of the shore. Three courageous sailors finally did ump out into the dark waters of the night. Fortunately, the boat used to bring these men to safety was maintained by the competent and experienced Isaac Small.

Another Life Saving oar boat remained near the *Trumbell* to see if they could help. Their twenty-two-foot-long oared boat overturned. In all, three surfmen agents perished in the ordeal, but every member of the *Trumbell* was rescued.

Stories of the USLSS (United States Life Saving Service), a precursor of today's Coast Guard, were both extraordinarily horrifying as they were courageous. Knowing that perhaps the next call to duty might be the final call to duty. Small stayed for decades protecting men from Cape Cod.

Truro Life Saving Station. (Old Harbor Life, Cape Cod, National Park Service.)

Wellfleet

Origin of the Town's Name

Incorporated from the North Precinct of Eastham, the town was originally named Poole for a seaport in Dorsetshire, a site famous for hosting the Parliamentary armies during their civil war. However, this name did not prove to be popular with the residents. So, it was changed to Wellfleet for two specific reasons. First, the term is closely sounding to the phrase a "whale fleet" of men who made a comfortable living by forging the acquisition of whale bones and sperm oil. In addition, it has an eerie resemblance to the looks of the Wellfleet oyster beds found within their British homeland.

A Brief History

The area residing within the limits of today's Wellfleet was originally part of a land grant by the Court of New Plymouth to "those that goe to dwell at Nossett" (Eastham). This land grant was made in 1644 and later extended in 1654 and 1674 to include virtually every part of the Outer Cape. Before 1644, the colonists of Plymouth and Duxbury delighted in the rich fishing grounds found in Wellfleet Harbor. This discovery led people to refer to the entire area surrounding these waters as Billingsgate, after the famous London fish market. The first permanent settlement in this area was made in the 1650s, and the number of dispersed separate dwellings slowly increased.

Wellfleet was part of neighboring Eastham until 1763 when it finally achieved unique town status after nearly thirty years of petitioning. Wellfleet's oyster beds drove the early economy, as did whaling and fishing. The town was home to as many as 30 whaling ships during the American Revolution.

Notable Connection to the Sea

In Wellfleet, mackerel fishing came to rule by the early nineteenth century. The town's whale fleet had been destroyed during the Revolution due to the British closing off the Cape Cod harbors. Fishermen learned that the mackerel traveled north in the early spring, providing an ample and profitable fishing season from April to October.

Many schooners were built in the Duck Creek shipyard. It was the largest whaling port in the country before the American Revolution. The first whaling schooner built in Wellfleet was the *Freemason*, built on Bound Brook Island in 1800. As a business enterprise started by Henry Rogers and sons, the family was responsible for building eight schooners: *Semeon Baker, JY Baker, JS Higgs, Benjamin Baker, RR Freeman, I H Horton, George Shattuck,* and *Varnum H Hill.* They were all were built within Wellfleet harbor.

Between the years 1860 and 1864, Wellfleet mackerel fishermen contributed as much as ten percent of the capture of this fish for the commonwealth. For example, the total value of the mackerel catch for Massachusetts was $2,251,065, with Wellfleet making up eleven percent of the total. The annual value of the town's catch for that year was over 27,350 fish. A large portion of this money earned stayed right in the town.

According to the 1860 census records, 284 males out of the 555 male population listed their occupation as a mariner or master mariner. If you also included occupations such as coopers, ship carpenters, fish inspectors, and other related jobs, we see that easily over half of the town was strongly connected to the sea.

LORENZO DOW BAKER (1840–1908)
Introduced the Love for Tropical Fruit to the USA

A successful West Indies trader Captain Baker discovered one specific product that would enrich him immensely. In 1870, after several years of general coasting, he made a trip to the South American tropics, first stopping in Venezuela and Brazil. He was captain of the schooner the *Telegraph*, which brought mining machinery to the Ciudad Bolivar on the Orinoco River. His return cargo was a shipment of Bamboo from Jamaica.

Almost as an afterthought, while at Port Moran, Baker thought that a curious new fruit called the "banana" mighty be an interesting acquisition. He was just testing the market and wondered if this food would be a curiosity to the New York City market, so he brought several bunches back home. This fruit went over so well that the next year, still using the *Telegraph*, he brought an entire cargo from Port Antonio, Jamaica, back to Boston. This marked the first time this fruit was ever delivered here in this level of quantity to New England.

He was shipping or moving bananas from the West Indies to Boston and Philadelphia for the next decade. The demand was extremely high, proving that a new product all by itself could result in the building of an empire. His wealth allowed him to construct two new vessels, the *Ruth N. Atwood* and the *Eunice P. Newcomb*, both coming out of Wellfleet. At times, he would skipper these trips himself, or at a minimum, he would hire a competent captain to bring these goods to Boston.

The major challenge for the banana importer was to get the highly perishable fruit to their delivery point before spoilage. He experimented with a range of safeguards combined with shipping speed that made the operation most profitable. In 1881, he partnered with his brother-in-law Elisha Hopkins to form the LD Baker and Co shipping company. Four years after that, he joined forces with Andrew Preston and eight other prominent capitalists to form the Boston Fruit Company. After a succession of other mergers and partnerships, the new shipping name would eventually become the United Fruit Company which finally became Chiquita Brands International.

By 1895, the corporation owned 40,000 acres of land and thirty-five different plantations growing fruit in the tropics. Before 1883, the Jamaica bananas were transported in schooners to the Northeast, but a steamer was soon added for its greater speed. In 1887 four steamers were running by the first of March, beginning a month earlier in the growing season than in the past. To this day, steamships are still used for this same purpose.

In 1886 before the acquisition of the supply chains, it was unheard of for a company to deal with shipping in this manner. Captain Baker would spend a long period living in Jamaica, cultivating the product, hiring and training new staff, and overseeing the cultivation of the crop.

Lorenzo Dow Baker's plantation. (Courtesy the United Fruit Company.)

Based on his methods, the quality of the delivered product improved every year. To this day, many of these business practices have been copied by other growers to expedite a fresh delivery system to port.

His business acquaintances and wealthy connections would more than once listen to his tales of the beauty of Cape Cod. Wellfleet would soon become a region of second homes for several successful investors living in the Boston, New York, and Philadelphia areas. He launched the modern banana production industry and, in the process, headquartered Boston's "Long Wharf" as the center of the tropical fruit trade along with the avocado pear. The latter fruit, ordinarily pear-shaped, is as large as an English pound pear and weighs from one to two pounds. The fruit is generally green when ripe, but sometimes it is streaked, making it a colorful sight.

CAPTAIN ELISHA DOANE (1699–1756)
The Battle of Louisburg

Elisha Doane decided to settle in Wellfleet (formerly Eastham) as a very young man. He married Hannah and purchased a small tract of land not far from the sea. After contemplating an option to farm, he faced the reality that arable land was anything but abundant while the prospect of ocean depths offered a much higher rate of return. As a whaler, he could realize a sizable fortune not only by paying off his debts to the local investor but also by keeping sufficient funds to expand his whaling options.

He was a deeply religious man and was asked to serve as a deacon in the Congregational Church established in Wellfleet in 1730. He continued to serve in this capacity for the duration of his life. When the Seven Year War (British name) emerged between Britain and France, American interests were protected with participation in the French and Indian War (American name). On February 20, 1774, Elisha Doane was commissioned as Captain of the 4th Co.7th Mass. Regiment. Under the command of Colonel Gorham, a contingent of Barnstable men, many with their families, traveled to Cape Breton in Nova Scotia. The battle of Louisburg unfolded to see whether British or French control of the Saint Lawrence Seaway would prevail.

The battle was fierce, with Captain Doane acknowledged as one of the true heroes of this contest. While serving in this pre-revolutionary war, he held that the personal interests of Barnstable County would be fortified with the British soldiers in charge as compared to having neighboring French colonists just to the north. While serving in Canada, it is believed that his daughter Ruth died at Cape Breton and his son Elisha Jr. was by his side serving as an ensign in the military.

The composite result of his honorable service to this local region had in no way benefited him financially. Since there were no spoils of war to be gained due to the final formal military agreement, he petitioned the court of Massachusetts to expand the use of reimbursement for acquiring arms, weapons, and governmental supplies. He was paid five pounds per month for his valiant work in securing these valuables. The high court finally granted this request to honor him and his men.

In an act of ironic twists, much of the credit for his war efforts were initially and incorrectly attributed to his father, who never made this trip due to his reaching the advanced age of seventy-three. In 1747, French and Indian troops arrived at Grand Pre at the Nova Scotia Fort, capturing all the Barnstable men stationed there. He was held as a captive and was weakened almost to death.

In a move of unusual proportion, he was used as collateral for the exchange of Rachel Quackenbush, who had been stolen by the Indians and purchased by the French. His name appears on an account posted in 1748, paid to the Minas prisoners from Canada. The efforts of these brave men from Barnstable County were responsible for Britain to take control of Canada and to force the French colonists to flee to the north to acquiesce to British rule.

He was eventually known as "King Doane" by the local people of Barnstable. His military sword had his name engraved and is still proudly held in possession by his descendants. He died in 1759 in his hometown and was buried with his surviving spouse at the extraordinary age of nine-five. His tombstone can still be viewed at the Duck Creek Burial Ground with the inscription "A deacon for thirty years, a commissioned officer, and an accomplished mariner has received the commission of Lieutenant Colonel for his reduction of Canada—Pray, think of me as you pass by."

In 1771, Wellfleet had thirty whaling vessels, each weighing no less than seventy-five tons and employing a minimum of fifteen men. It appears as if these ships started out in the early spring and then went to the Gulf of Guinea in Western Africa, returning in the Fall. They remained stored in Wellfleet for the winter. In 1771 Captain Elisha Duane had a fortune of over 120,000 pounds, making him one of the richest men in Massachusetts. Nonetheless, the Revolutionary War greatly diminished the overall wealth of Wellfleet men. Many sea-faring men were seized by the British and died on prison ships or removed to Penobscot or other places. The whaling industry never restored itself to its once prominent status.

CAPTAIN GEORGE BAKER (1822–1895)
Captain of the Fishing Schooner, the Maria Theresa

He was born in 1822 in a small town located in the Alsace region of France. His original name, at birth, was Balthasar Conrad. Being an orphan, he was graciously taken into Centre d'Enfants.

At the age of eleven, in 1833, a religious organization decided to move him to Boston via a merchant vessel. Even at this very young age, he loved the ocean experience feeling very comfortable with the ebb and flow of the cresting waves. Two years later, his presence came to attention to the Baker family in Wellfleet. Although himself not an extremely wealthy man, David Baker made a very good profit in the fishing industry.

David, the future father of Lorenzo Baker, was now responsible for the education and training of his adopted son, George Baker. As a youth, he lived on Griffins Island with Isiah and Hannah Baker and was a precocious active youth. His dad, David, owned a shipping vessel named the *Leonidas* which sailed out of Duck Harbor, mostly searching for the mackerel and other smaller fish. His apprenticeship was an active one as George soon mastered the ocean trends, the fishing trends, and the process necessary to capture mackerel expediently

By the age of twenty, he had learned such a proficient degree of details that he took command of his first ship, the *Tiara*. His immediate success allowed him to marry Mercy Higgins, another Wellfleet native. In his mid-twenties, his newly acquired wealth found him searching for a larger ship. He placed his capital into the construction of the *Maria Theresa*. This new ship constructed in Wellfleet was personalized to host ornate features such as an enlarged wrench and advanced netting and trapping. He proudly took command as the first captain to command a seventy-ton, two-masted fishing and coasting schooner.

In the 1840s, mackerel fishing reached its heyday in Wellfleet and other seacoast towns. It was noted that in 1845, over sixty vessels were operating out of the Wellfleet harbors. Most of these fishing ships were known as the "Pinkie Type." These vessels were distinctive in their appearance and common style, capturing the imagination of the American Maritime Art scene. "Pinkie" means that the stern is "pinked" or somewhat blended or pinched together, coming from a corruption of a Dutch word. Hand-line fishing seemed to be the order of the day.

George Baker would captain eight other schooners in the fishing, oyster hauling, and packet transportation system. His entrepreneurial interests would expand to the lumber, coal, and building supply company in his later life. He would become a trustee of the local bank, an officer in the Marine Benevolent Society, and even serve as the local town tax collector. At the age of sixty-two, George Baker enthusiastically claimed the title of a naturalized United States citizen at a US district court in Boston. Fifty-one years after arriving in a new country, he appreciated the distinct honor of being called an American citizen.

A Pinkie schooner with its unique sail formation. (Courtesy Digital Commonwealth Collection.)

JOHN MASHOW (1805–1885)
Born a Slave and Became a Master Shipbuilder

The great shipping fleet of Wellfleet in the early 1800s had to be built. One of the least known but perhaps among the prime ship designers of this era was John Mashow. He was born in 1805 because of a union between a slave and a South Carolina planter. Being a very good student, showing promise as a very able carpentry worker, he was noticed by John Michaux, a local shipbuilder. He took John into his care, allowing him to apprentice in the shipyards of South Carolina.

When his father died in 1815, there was a provision in the planter's will that his adopted son would become a free man upon his death. His next ship tutor had even more of a solid reputation in the maritime world. Laban Thacher had constructed many coastal vessels used by the southern fleet. By the age of 27, his renown as a shipbuilder had reached such a level that he was able to strike out on his own. His journey up north to Massachusetts permitted him even more opportunities as demand for new and bigger ships was certainly in demand in that region.

Laban Thatcher was a greatly respected merchant in his era. Much of his work involved the construction of boatyards, ships, and even whole villages. Laban established the quant village of Padanaram (also known as South Dartmouth) as a reference to a biblical figure.

John worked for Laban Thatcher designing merchant vessels for the next twenty-eight years. In acquiring his new location near New Bedford, he could claim twenty-eight fishing schooners, nineteen whalers, and two sloops as fully completed at his site on the Apponagansett River. Wellfleet sailors requested one-third of these ships. One of his master ship creations was the *Maria Theresa*, with design input given to him by Captain George Baker.

One reason why fishing became such a profitable industry for Wellfleet sailors was the greater speed and customized cargo space that a newer well-designed ship could offer. As a ship architect, he paid great attention to finer lines and sharper bows with a larger sail area. These features contributed to constructing a more competitive larger, and faster schooner able to haul larger commercial products to market. These newly built ships were used for coasting on the Eastern shore or hauling oysters to the Boston Market.

As a student of ship architecture, John often first carved a half-model of the schooner's hull. Then he transferred lines from the sections of his model, creating an appropriate mold for shaping each of the vessel's oak frames. His building techniques were both innovative and cost-efficient. His genius and creative joy brought joy to the owners of the shipbuilding industry. He was in great demand but stayed where he was, often consulting with Captain George Baker of Wellfleet.

In his shipyard, he supervised a crew of sixteen shipwrights and carpenters. They would lay the keel and bow, cut and raise each frame, and attach the planking so each ship would be a durable seaworthy schooner or whaler.

His ships were particularly attractive to the Baker family. Records indicate that David Baker captained the *Baker* while *Maria Theresa* was the pride of George Baker. The ability to customize the exact details of a fishing ship based upon a captain's requests was a unique situation for this day and age.

His life was profitable, contributing to the rise of the shipping industry in the Wellfleet region. He became a proud father to five sons who proudly called themselves whalers. Based on the written acclaims and notes from the New Bedford Whaling Museum, a ship architect committee awarded him the title of "the most important African-American figure involved in shipbuilding design."

Image of boats designed near New Bedford in 1867.

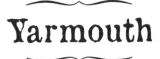

Yarmouth

Origin of the Town's Name

There are two potentially different versions of the origin of the town's name. Some historians believe that the Pilgrims first embarked from Leyden, Holland, from the port of Yarmouth, England, on the first leg of their journey to find religious freedom in the new world. While a more modern opinion is that the plentiful supply of alewife fish in the new province at the "mouth of the Yar River" reminded the settlers of English boaters of a very common site in the Yar River area, In the very early days, the northwest section of Yarmouth was called Mattachese, the northeast part was known as Hockanom while lands along Lewis Bay were referred to as the South Sea.

A Brief History

Yarmouth was incorporated as part of the Plymouth Colony on September 3, 1639. The settlement was led by John Crowe (later spelled Crowell), Thomas Howes, and Anthony Thatcher. Along with Sandwich and Barnstable, the town is one of the oldest towns incorporated on Cape Cod. Yarmouth originally included a portion of land that is now Dennis. Dennis later separated as a community on June 19, 1793.

From 1642 to 1645, Yarmouth furnished soldiers for the Plymouth Colony's expeditions against the Narragansett skirmishes occurring throughout Southern New England. In 1648, the Plymouth Colony's legislature appointed Myles Standish through the General Court to adjudicate any existing land disputes among the Yarmouth settlers. Fifteen Yarmouth men participated in the Great Swamp Fight of King Phillip's War. Yarmouth troops also saw service in the early years of King Williams

War. In the early eighteenth century, based on their beneficial military service, many industrious Yarmouth veterans who fought in these wars were granted lands on the Cape and settlements in Gorham, Maine.

Notable Connection to the Sea

Today, a very visible feature of the great respect and reverence paid to their former sea captains was recognizing vast numbers of historic homes located within the town. The Historical Society of Old Yarmouth very carefully identified the homes of the several captains living in the northern part of Yarmouth. Through their earnest painstaking research through town records, over fifty homes have been documented as an official residence of a former sea captain. Hence, The Captains' Mile was established and still exists today. This delineated trail of maritime history identifies the former residences of seafaring men. It proclaims their presence on maps and brochures. In addition, each home, now all privately owned, is marked with a certifying plaque easily discernible with a distinctive oval-shaped black and gold border.

One of these homes, the house of Captain Bangs Halley, has been conserved for historic purposes and is now used as a cite for many events of the Yarmouth Historical Society. Across the street from this site, you will find the Elephant Home, also a two-hundred-year-old captain's house. This site was both the residence and the worksite of Edward Gorey. Gorey was a celebrated artist and illustrator. A brief synopsis of each captain's sailing history is encapsulated with data placed on a popular brochure and is easily obtainable from any internet search or the local town's historical society.

The town celebrates its nautical heritage with the names of sea captains on several consecutive roads on Station Avenue as one journeys from Cape Cod Bay to the Long Island Sound. Just below Route 28, near the Bass River bridge, a second Captain's Mile with a large enclave of sea captains' homes is also being researched. The Judah Baker Windmill in South Yarmouth is itself historic all to itself. The frequent repositioning of this windmill relates directly to the lives of the shipmasters. For each of its relocations, a sea captain's family was prominently responsible.

Captain Judah Baker first had the original windmill constructed in 1791 in North Dennis to grind corn. It was then sold to Captain

Freeman Crowell, who transferred it to East Dennis to accommodate the local demand for flour. Finally, Captain Braddock Mathews transported it to its present location in South Yarmouth on the banks of the Bass River. Its location assisted the local community when his son Seth operated a general store contiguous to the mill.

CAPTAIN ASA ELDRIDGE (1809–1856)
The Finest and Perhaps Premiere Cape Cod Mariner

Henry Kittridge, the cape Cod maritime historian, boasts of "Asa Eldridge as the most distinguished shipmaster that the Cape has ever produced and is among the world's half-dozen greatest shipmasters" This illustrious proclamation comes from an author who perhaps has the most extensive knowledge of famous sea captains. The quality of his research is immediately evident in his book, *Cape Cod: Its History and Its People*.

In 1829, Asa succeeded his brother as captain of the brig *America*. His was a ship designed for carrying cargo to a wide variety of ports. On his first trip as captain, at the age of twenty, he took the ship from New York to Savannah to Liverpool. His next trip followed a similar route but included New Orleans. This trip was followed by a round-trip voyage to Russia, returning via Denmark. It is noted that on the return trip, his ship was greatly ravaged by storms, prompting him to secure a Seaman's Protection Certificate.

Seamen's Protection Certificates were usually printed documents, varying in size and style, carried by American seamen as proof of citizenship and authenticity of ownership. The individual shipowner obtained the certificate through the customhouse, public notary, or U.S. Consul as required to enter a foreign port. It contained the person's name, birthplace, approximate age, height, skin color, eye and hair color, and other distinctive descriptive information, such as the location of scars or tattoos. "United States of America" was often printed prominently across the top of the document with the word "protection" added.

In the first half of the nineteenth century, Liverpool, England, had become perhaps the world's largest seaport open to carry trades around the globe. Initially, its location was the first leg of the infamous slave trade. In the first step, products such as textiles, ironware, and weapons went to the West Coast of Africa. At that point, the captains bartered for slaves, bringing the enslaved people to the West Indies. The sale of the slaves would then allow for the purchase of tobacco, sugar, and cotton, which then ventured back to Liverpool to complete the triangle.

After the British Slave Trade Act of 1807, a new type of cargo was needed due to the disallowance of carrying of oppressed people. Textile mills became the day's rage, creating new commerce leading to the Industrial Revolution. Spinning jennies and other weaving types of looms became a new desirable product. Since the southern states of America never heavily pursued maritime expansion, there was a need for

Clipper calling card of the Red Jacket, *named after Captain Eldridge.*

Northern vessels to bring textiles with related equipment and products to their shore. Captain Eldridge was at the right spot at the right time to be of service.

Captain Eldridge amassed an impressive reputation and great wealth. With this new type of technology available, Southern states had an incentive to grow cotton and demand manpower to gather it. Now it possessed appropriate equipment to establish a cotton trade with Northern states. In 1854, Captain Eldridge guided his clipper ship, the *Red Jacket*, to many lucrative ports of call. His ship's name was taken from a term for a Native American warrior.

This masterful ship was designed for grace and speed. In one voyage, he went from New York and to Liverpool in only thirteen days, 1 hour, and twenty-five minutes, dock to dock, setting a speed record for the fastest trans-Atlantic crossing by a commercial sailing vessel. It remained as an unbroken record for a clipper ship ever since.

Eldridge is also known for captaining Cornelius Vanderbilt's private steam-powered yacht, the *North Star*. The tycoon often took a small group of family and friends on summer cruises around Europe in 1853.

His connection with E. K. Collins resulted in forming a shipping indus-try, which eventually grew to become the Cunard Steamship Lines.

In 1856, Captain Eldridge's good fortune gave out as he skippered the steamship SS *Pacific*. His ship fully disappeared at sea on a voyage from Liverpool to New York. The SS *Pacific* was a wooden sidewheel steamer built in 1849 for the American Collins line. There is no defini-tive evidence of how his ship suddenly disappeared, but it was lost at sea without a trace.

CAPTAIN LEVI BAKER (1803–1864)
An Opponent of The Slave Inspection Act

A Virginia law passed in 1856 demanded that every ship heading North must be searched for the possibility of run-away slaves being on board. If the vessel sailed north without the benefit of inspection, the captain was required to pay a fee of $500. They also had to pay a fee of five dollars for ordinary vessels and two dollars for coal-carrying boats for the privi-lege of undergoing this inspection. If the payment to the court was not addressed, the ship could be seized. This law realized a generous profit for the government of $137,000 during its first year of implementation.

The small fee was deemed a nuisance, but most sea-faring men agreed to pay this nominal sum to transact business. Captain Levi Baker, how-ever, challenged the constitutionality of this statute. He was a twenty-five-year veteran of sailing through Southern ports. In July of 1856, he was both the commander and owner of the schooner *N.C. Hall*. He lay at anchor at Hampton, Virginia, with a cargo of corn and fruit bound for New Bedford.

A pilot boat approached and asked him of his intended direction. No visual inspection of his vessel ever ensued despite giving a truthful response. Fearing that the fruit had a limited shelf life and seeing a favorable wind emerge, the fearful captain threw caution to the wind and took up to depart. He honestly believed that some other smaller pilot boater would eventually enter his path to conduct the necessary search. No pilot boat was visible, and his cargo was perishable, so he decided to put out to sea.

A month later, his boat, the *N.C. Hall*, was back in Norfolk with a new captain in charge. Captain Baker was held detained in Massachusetts as the vessel's owner. The ship was now in the custody of the state of Virginia, having transgressed the commonwealth's maritime codes. He received permission to return to Virginia to advocate for his vessel's release. By now, the fines had reached a total of $700. Capitan Baker was above all a prudent businessman who decided that paying the fee was better than risking the full loss of his ship cargo valued at a total worth of over $3000. He also completed an analysis of the ship's status to determine that keeping the ship away from the sea for too long would most likely result in worms making the vessel unnavigable.

He took it upon himself to go to every Virginian legal official to obtain a release and pay this fee. No court officer, state representative, or port official would even speak to him. He was even encouraged by some Virginia lawyers, but they had no jurisdiction in the matter. They believed that this law was most likely unconstitutional and should be challenged. Even the state's Governor Wise failed to intervene in the matter.

In effect, he was unable to recover the ship while Virginia condemned it. It was sold at a public auction for a fee of $750. Returning home and

A sketch of a slave auction titled "Slave Auction in the South: The Weeping Time," by Theordore Davis. (Courtesy of Lasalle University.)

feeling dejected, he now took on this decision as a personal challenge. He would fight this unjust law on behalf of all the Eastern shippers. He petitioned the Massachusetts legislature to contest this treatment to a higher court level. His request was granted, with the state awarding him $2,500 to fight this injustice at the federal level.

However, the sad yet unfortunate truth was that by the time the US Supreme Court was set to hear the arguments, our nation became embroiled in a Civil War, and there were much more important courts cases that demanded their attention. This case was left on the docket and was never officially adjudicated. This captain fell victim to the vicissitudes of slavery, federal unrest, and inconsistent maritime practices.

ICHABOD PADDOCK (1687–1750)
Instrumental in Nantucket Whaling

Ichabod Paddack (original spelling) was born to Zachariah Paddack and Deborah Sears Paddack in Yarmouth. As a youth, he had earned a steady reputation as a trainer of the craft of whaling. One of his specific educational concepts was the utilization of specialized speedy boats. In those early days, rather than venturing out far into the ocean, shore whaling entailed a process where spotters along the beach would call out with smaller boats to pursue their prey quickly. These boats were twenty feet long with a double bow to facilitate quick and facile navigation. The crew consisted of six men. Each crew member had a specific task: turning, spotting, coaching, or spearing.

Nantucket, in the 1690s, was looking for exactly this type of industry to arrive on its island. The island was not seen as a viable agricultural site due to its sandy land texture, yet there was a desire to expand commerce. The three Paddock brothers, Ichabod, Joseph, and Nathaniel, all arrived onshore simultaneously. Ichabod's mission was to train the local citizenry to capture whales most expediently. In that era, the indigenous people far outnumbered the European population, quickly becoming the highest number of trained sailors.

A system was created in which the Aquinnah people, a subset of the Wampanoag nation, could purchase food and necessary supplies from the white settlers on credit. This ability to keep people in a state of debt was the perfect vehicle to form a continuing labor pool of local young indigenous whalers willing to work off their debt to sustain their families.

There were several legends and myths touted about Ichabod's life. Some stories involved seeing mermaids, while another described a precursor of the *Moby Dick* story as he was known to chase often a large whale named Crooked Jaw. Legend has it that he eventually captured the beast with a specially prepared harpoon given to him by his wife. Despite the probable fictional aspects of his life, scores of young men were certainly directly trained by him to become accomplished whalers. Based on his poor sense of morality and visible poor behavior, many of the Nantucket Quakers grew uneasy with his disposition and excessive drinking, finally asking him to leave the island.

The commerce of whaling now put Nantucket on the map. The high demand for whale oil kept New England lamps burning bright for over a century. There are records of more than two hundred whaling ships traveling out of Nantucket that created the required commerce that was desired.

Unfortunately for Ichabod, his inclination towards drinking and chasing women did not sit well with many of the local Quakers who wanted a better example to be set. He was ultimately demanded to return to the mainland. However, his two brothers, Joseph and Nathaniel, remained with the residents and prospered.

CAPTAIN JOHN SEARS (1744–1817)
The Sleepy Captain Who Envisioned the Saltwork Process

In the colonial era, salt was an essential need to preserve meats and fish. It was a typical and constant process to place perishable foods into barrels filled with almost equal amounts of salt and fish. This mixture would trigger the salt to remove any moisture. The fish could be placed into clean barrels and shipped out to any destination when completely dry. Originally, salt would arrive from Liverpool, England. A higher grade of Mediterranean salt was also cultivated in caved-in sea areas. When Great Britain imposed their infamous tax on tea, they also imposed a significant increase on the price of salt.

When the war began, Cape Cod families were severely hampered by the lack of available salt. Not only was the cost of salt inflated, but

British-controlled waters would also embargo any incoming vessels from Europe, often seizing control of its shipment. There was no safe way for local fishermen to bring their daily catches to market.

Demand became so fierce that the Continental Congress passed a reward system paying a supplemental fee of thirty-three cents per bushel for any salt delivery. Now a strong incentive system for local salt drove a sort of contest. An early attempt was to boil four hundred gallons of seawater, but it used two cords of wood to produce only one bushel of salt, which was seen as ineffective.

A Yarmouth-born sea captain, "Sleepy" John Sears, came to the rescue. His nickname was acquired by his noticeable habit of frequently staring into space during a conversation. Rather than being narcoleptic, his condition seemed to be one of persistent focus. He made his primary living as a merchant ship captain. His first attempt at salt production was called Sears' Folly by his neighbors. He filled a shallow wooden vat using manual labor to fill up the water. His initial offering was a mere eight bushels of salt.

In 1778, he improved his concept by filtering out ocean water with the help of a large bilge pump into tightly caulked vats to eliminate spillage. His cousin, Rueben Sears, improved this process even more. A rolling roof was invented, allowing for an opening into the sunshine. This design would keep out unwanted rainwater as necessary. Closing the vats at night kept dew from tempering the enclosed salt in the morning. Another cousin, Nathaniel Freeman, designed a way to use a windmill to pump the water from the sea. Finally, a very cost-efficient manner to produce salt was available in Cape Cod.

By 1837, there were over 650 saltworks producing close to twenty-six tons per year. Saltworks existed in every town in Cape Cod. If you ever pass by any current street named "Saltworks Road," you know you are close to history. Once salt deposits were discovered in upstate New York, the industry suffered a rapid reduction of need; however, salt production continued its operation for forty more years.

When Captain Sears died in 1817, he was a very wealthy man. He was buried in Brewster. During the War of 1812, the British cannons threatened to destroy many of the larger saltworks, exerting an exorbitant

A Cape Cod windmill used in production of salt. (Windmill Driven Saltwords, Digital Collection.)

ransom fee to preserve them. The town of Brewster capitulated to the payment while Orleans bravely defied the menace.

ALLEN HINCKLEY KNOWLES (1814–1875)
A Frequent Crosser of the Cape of Good Hope

Captain Allen H. Knowles is perhaps best noted by the members of the Yarmouth Historical Society for his house swap in 1863. The other party in that swap was Captain Bangs Hallet, who traded his residence. Today, the Hallet House is the center of the Yarmouth Historical Society and its

Museum. Knowles, throughout his sailing days, became a most distinguished mariner.

Allen Hinckley Knowles was born in Eastham in 1814, the first of his parents' six children. Even by Cape Cod's nautical standards, his family was particularly associated with the sea, claiming five sea captains: Allen's father, Allen himself, and three of his four brothers were all captains.

The ships his father was sailing belonged to one of Boston's most ambitious shipowners, Benjamin Bangs, who in 1840 took on Allen as a captain as well. Over the next seven years, the younger Knowles commanded four different ships for Bangs: *Henry Lee, Coquimbo, Sophia,* and *Edward Everett.* He completed five roundtrip jaunts between Boston and Valparaiso and two to Europe—one to Italy and another to Liverpool.

The voyages to Chile were especially long, typically taking about ten months, which meant that Knowles' wife Mary and their two young children had to endure lengthy periods without him. During one such period, in May 1842, Mary died in childbirth, along with the newborn. Knowles did not learn of the tragedy until December, over six months later, when he finally arrived back in Boston.

Death in childbirth was undoubtedly common in those times. (remove quickly) Allen Knowles did not re-marry until 1849, seven years after Mary's death. He acquired a new position as a captain of a transatlantic packet ship sailing between Boston and Liverpool, with roundtrips completed in under three months.

His transition to this role had occurred the previous year. Shortly after, he took command of a new ship for Benjamin Bangs, the *Robert C Winthrop.* Enoch Train, another prominent Boston shipowner, expanded the packet line to Liverpool and persuaded Bangs to lease him the new ship. Liverpool was then the chief English port for trade with the US and the principal destination for most transatlantic packet lines. It was also the main point of embarkation for thousands of emigrants fleeing Ireland to escape the Great Famine.

During three voyages for Train on the *Robert C Winthrop*, Knowles transported over 650 survivors from Liverpool to Boston. On the last voyages, he was accompanied by his second wife, Caroline, whom he had married just days before.

After making that switch in 1849, Knowles took command first of the *Western Star* and then the *Chariot of Fame*. Both assignments were influenced by a major event in the year before his switch: the discovery of gold in California. Suddenly, legions of would-be prospectors wanted to sail as quickly as possible to San Francisco, a voyage of more than 15,000 miles that included the treacherous passage around Cape Horn.

In June 1853, Knowles moved to the ship representing the pinnacle of his career, the *Chariot of Fame*. She was one of two identical clipper ships built for Enoch Train by Donald McKay, perhaps the most famous shipbuilder in our country's history. With a cargo capacity of 2050 tons, she was over five times bigger than Knowles' first command, the *Henry Lee*. Her size had advantages and challenges. She could assuredly carry more passengers and valuable goods, yet; she needed a larger crew and was harder to fill up with cargo for outbound voyages to Liverpool.

By then, Knowles had already detached himself and the *Chariot of Fame* to pursue a distinctly less glamorous but more profitable business. Renewing his acquaintance with Cape Horn, he began sailing to the Chincha Islands off the coast of Chile to load up with guano, the dried excrement of sea birds that, in the days before agrochemicals, was in great demand as a fertilizer. He completed his third such voyage in 1860 and was then forced from the high seas for five years by the Civil War. At least this gave him plenty of time to devote to his house-swap with Bangs Hallet in 1863. During this enforced layoff, he and Caroline also had the last of their three children.

But in 1866, he was back, commencing an eight-year relationship with yet another Boston shipowner, Elijah Williams. This saw him command the *Puritan*, *Agenor*, and *Conqueror*, making nine more voyages in total. The first seven took him to Liverpool, with stops at intermediate ports for cargoes—usually New Orleans or St. John, but on one occasion San Francisco, and on another, both Callao (in Chile, for guano) and Savannah (for cotton). The eighth was his last voyage around Cape Horn,

Deciding to retire to Yarmouth and stay away from the sea proved to be a bit challenging for him. As he ventured out for a smaller fishing adventure one final time, he suffered a stroke, dying a few months later.

References

Anthology Collection, *Three Centuries of the Cape Cod County*, Barnstable, Massachusetts, 1685–1985, Published by Barnstable County.

Allison, Robert, (2010) A Short History of Cape Cod, Commonwealth Editions.

Author Unknown, (August 1995) "Sleepy John Sears and the Revolutionary White Gold of Cape Cod," retrieved from: www.newenglandhistoricalsociety.com/sleepy.john.

Barnard, Ruth (1975), *A History of Early Orleans*, Sullwold Publishing, sponsored by the Orleans Historical Society, Taunton, Massachusetts.

Albert, George, The *Captain's Wife* (1946): The Diary of Didama Kelley Doane of West Harwich wife of Uriel Doane, a two-year voyage, Syracuse University Press, Syracuse, New York.

Beckmann, Nils, Peleg Nye (2014), *The Jonah of Cape Cod*, CreateSpace Independent Publishing Platform, North Charleston, South Carolina.

Brigham. Perry (1920), *Cape Cod and the Old Colony*, Putnam and Sons, New York City, New York.

Coogan, James and Sheedy, Jack, (2001) *Cape Cod Voyage, A Journey through Cape Cod's History and Lore*, Harvest Home Books, East Dennis, Massachusetts.

Coogan, James (2008) *Sail Away Ladies*, Harvest Home Books.

Composite Authorship, *Three Centuries in a Cape Cod Village*, The Story of Chatham, (2012), Chatham Historical Society, Schiffer Publishing, Philadelphia, Pennsylvania.

Green, Sachse, McCauley, 2006 *The Names of Cape Cod*, Arcadia Press, Republished by Commonwealth Editions, Carlisle, Massachusetts.

Huggins, Cynthia, (1977), *From Mastheads to Moorings: A Chronicle of Brewster Sea Captains*, Master' Dissertation, Boston College.

Husted, Nell (1979) *Here's Provincetown*, Notes and Interviews, published by the Provincetown Historical Society.

Jackman, S. W. (1979) *The Journal of William Sturgis*, Sono Nis Press, Victoria B.C., Canada.

Kittredge, Henry, (1935), *Shipmasters of Cape Cod*, Riverside Press, Houghton Mifflin Company, Boston, Massachusetts.

Lee, Roscoe (2013), "The Benjamin Fessenden Story," June 30, 2013, *Barnstable Patriot Ledger*, news article.

Lincoln, Joseph, *Cape Cod Yesterdays*, (1935) Cornwall Press, New York City, New York.

Mayo, Sarah Augusta (2003) (unpublished work edited by Janine Perry) *Looking Back, The Manuscript of Sarah Augusta Mayo*, 2003 – The Archives of the Brewster Ladies Library Association.

Miles, V. (2015), *The Lost Hero of Cape Cod*, Captain Asa Eldridge, and the Maritime Trade that Shaped America, Historical Society of Old Yarmouth Press, Yarmouthport, Massachusetts.

Monreau, Mira, (2010) *A Home on the Rolling Deep,* the Stories of 78 Chatham Sea Captains, Transcribed and introduced, Chatham Historical Society Sponsor.

Nickerson, Joseph, and Geraldine, (2008), *Chatham Sea Captains in the Age of Sail,* History Press.

Paine, Jane, 2000, *Cape Cod Masters of the Sea,* extraordinary tales of Brewster's Shipmasters and sea captains, Wrack line Press, Boston, Massachusetts.

Paine, John et al (1977) Joint authorship by the Harwich Historical Commission, published by the Harwich Historical Commission.

Pre-Revolutionary Diaries, "Life of Benjamin Berry," Massachusetts On-Line Archival Records, retrieved on 4/24/2018.

Randall, Roger (1975) *Shipmasters of the First Parish in Brewster,* sponsored by the 275th Parish Celebration Committee, October 19, 1975.

Reid, Nancy (1996) *Dennis, Cape Cod from Firstcomers to Newcomers,* Dennis Historical Society Publication.

Sears. Joseph Henry (1906) *Brewster Shipmasters,* C.W. Swift Publisher, Yarmouthport, Massachusetts.

Sheedy, Jack (1995) *Dennis Journal of a Town,* Commissioned by the Dennis Bicentennial Commission.

Shockley, Megan (2010) *The Captain's Widow of Sandwich,* ebook citation, retrieved on May 2, 2020, NYPress9780814783191/the-captains-widow-of-Sandwich.

Thoreau, Henry David (2012 ed.) *Cape Cod,* Penguin Random House Press, New York City, New York.

Vital Records of the Town of Brewster, (1904) *Mayflower* Descendent Chart, edited by George Bowman.

About the Author

The first part of Michael Pregot's career was in preschool through high school public education. He has served as a world language teacher, an assistant principal, an elementary and high school principal, and a district-wide school superintendent. The second leg of his career was dedicated to higher education, where he worked as a graduate-level college professor of education, an assistant professor of school administration, and finally as a department chair of a school leadership program. He is still a part-time university instructor for the University of Georgia while residing in Cape Cod.

The third segment of his life work connects to his deep appreciation for Cape Cod. He has moved his attention to Cape Cod maritime studies. His first research project analyzed the thirty-six sea captains honored by name at each hole of the Captain's Golf Course. He completed this research project of local maritime figures for the benefit of Brewster town records.

As his research progressed through each of the fifteen Cape Cod historical societies and regional libraries, he saw the depth and richness of maritime lore scattered in every beach, hamlet, and village of the Cape. He concluded that a more comprehensive view of biographies of sea captains was an enticing field of study, where reviewing its historic past enriches the perspective of its present-day life.

For the past two years, he has provided both online and direct presentations on the life of notable Cape captains for various organizations such as public and private golf courses, historical societies, local clubs, town libraries, the National Park Service, and town environmental boards. The extensive depth of overall significant sea captain achievements and more localized points of curiosity on Cape Cod maritime material have captured his time, imagination, focus, and passion.